DAEMONS
OF FORTUNE

DAEMONS
OF FORTUNE

DAVID THOMPSON

✴ TRANS MUNDANE ✴
PUBLISHING
—— OCCULT KNOWLEDGE ——

A Legal Disclaimer:

By Law, I must let you know that this is for entertainment purposes only, and does not claim to prevent or cure any diseases. The advice in this book should not be construed as financial, medical, or psychological advice. Please seek such advice from a professional.

By purchasing this book, and working the rituals, you understand results are not guaranteed. Considering this and in the unlikely event that this course does not work for you or, in the very unlikely event, this book causes physical harm to you or a loved one, you agree that you will not hold David Thompson, our affiliates and employees liable for any damages you may experience or incur.

The author does not guarantee that the material in this book will ensure gambling success. By its very definition, gambling is risky.

Each individual's success depends on his or her background, dedication, desire, and motivation.

A Warning:

This is very powerful material. When worked properly, you may see unexpected results. These rituals and petitions are like electricity, the energy will flow toward the intended output. In saying this, please be firm in your intentions and make absolutely sure what you want is truly want you desire.

As they say, be careful what you wish for, you just might get it.

To my grandfather,
one of the luckiest guys I ever knew.

Scientists have calculated that the chances of something so patently absurd actually existing are millions to one. But magicians have calculated that million-to-one chances crop up nine times out of ten.

~~Terry Pratchett

PART ONE

Introduction

Fortune magick in sports and gambling is a real thing.

Go to any sports venue, during a major sports event, such as America's Cup, World Cup, USA's Super Bowl or College Football Playoffs, and you will see each bar or pub jammed with people watching the sports on TV, often wearing "lucky" shirts, hats, all in the hopes of causing their favorite team to win.

It is during these events when people will begin to send up prayers to any deity on listening duty for their team to prevail, regardless of personal opinions on religion.

Sometimes, a team that was not expected to even be in the event, manages to win against a stronger opponent, and their fans go wild. In televised interviews with these fans, you will hear or see evidence of prayers to various spiritual beings for this weaker team to have prevailed. It's as if their regular deity was replaced by a sports enthusiast deity who happened to favor that one team over the other.

Then the mask on that deity drops away, and we see a

mysterious figure emerge. Often this figure is feminine, always beyond beautiful, and she will always slip away the moment you notice her.

The Lady.

This book is about the magick of fortune and luck. I was researching "luck" spirits, and a result, I was taken to meet with this elusive goddess, all while meditating about which daemons I should summon about this book. Thus, she was added to this book project. Not because she demanded it.

No, this goddess never demands anything.
She expects it!

CHAPTER ONE

The Daemons of Fortune

This book is based, in part, on a class I gave a few years ago, Daemonic Money Magick. In this class, I introduced the concept of calling upon seven daemons all in one ritual. Summoning one after the other. Then they all show up, if only to see what all the fuss is about. Like people who're invited to a party, but aren't sure if they'll like it or even stay. So, they'll show up, hang around a while, then after a bit, they're dancing around and having a good time.

Along with that class, I also introduced a special sigil. This design has some serious power. The sigils for this book are even stronger.

As always, the sigils in this book will also be on my website, available as a download in both PDF and JPG formats.

The Process

What causes "good luck"? Lady Luck will often arrive and be behind you for no obvious reasons. My ***Fortuna*** book looks at ways to appease this illusive spirit, making sure luck stays with you.

For this magick method, I am defining Fortune as "luck in business, money affairs, investments, luck and fortune in your personal and public life."

There are some folks who are just naturally fortunate. Being in the appropriate place and time: sitting next to a well-known actor and striking up a conversation that results in the sale of a screenplay or when you are looking for a "angel investor" for a new business, you run into a wealthy investor at a casual meeting.

However, and you'll read the following statement multiple times in this book: ***I can't promise that the rituals in this book will help you improve your luck when playing games of chance.***

Nothing in this book will guarantee a shift in your luck. You may not win the lottery, and you might even lose money at a casino. Play responsibly.

There are rituals in this book to adjust your lucky aura, and this luck may manifest in ways *other than in gambling.* Lucky encounter with a potential employer, luck with getting that interview, luck with finding suitable life partners, and luck in most any other pursuit. Playing golf and scoring like a pro. Bowling a perfect game. Or simply luck at finding the best parking spot at the shopping mall right before a major holiday.

In this book, you'll be introduced to a Goddess, The Lady, and to a group of Goetic Daemons I call "The Seven". Seven is a mystical number and results from contacting several daemons and finding seven who said they'll be willing to be in this book and they will show up when summoned.

Tracking Your Results

I advise you to make notes on your magickal practices no matter what. Record the times you do each ritual in a simple notepad or journal. Include the ritual's name, the day and time you performed the ritual, the moon phase, and anything else that comes to mind.

By doing this, you could start to see a trend about the magic's working hours and optimal days. Record what you did differently and the outcomes if you vary from the written process.

Only by doing this can you track what does, and doesn't, work for you.

Magick is a personal journey. What works for me might not work 100% for you.

(*Magick journals exist, and I even offer one. Search online for High Magick 101 Workbook and Ritual Log.)

Personally, I often just use a cheap school spiral notebook, and I'd write notes during and after the ritual. Then I could track the magick. This is important, and I'll let you know why in the next section, but for now, I want to impress upon you the need to track your magick.

Most magick is subtle. It'll gently nudge you in the right

direction if you are sensitive enough to listen.

As I was writing this book, and working out the rituals and path workings, I took detailed notes. I would hear Bune, or The Lady, guide me in writing the rituals, making sure I was getting all the details needed for each step. I'd track the results and make corrections, seeing what worked. And what didn't work.

Sending me the images I'd need to craft the sigils, and correct any mistakes when I'd sketch out the sigil. This continued even when I wasn't in the ritual as I'd draw the sigil in my drawing program.

Why is it important for you to track your results? Well...

Acknowledge the Power

There is a list of Rules for the Earth making its rounds on the internet. Called the "The Eleven Satanic Rules of the Earth", it comes to us via the Satanic Church, and is written by Anton Szandor LaVey, published in 1967. (I guess it's the counter-argument for the ten commandments.)

One rule, Rule #7, stood out to me.

It read: "Acknowledge the power of magick if you have employed it successfully to obtain your desires. If you deny the power after having called upon it, you will lose all you have obtained."

This is absolutely the truth. I have seen this happen so many, many times.

Acknowledge the power. Thank the power.

I've seen what happens when magic fails and someone blames magic or a deity for it failing; everything they try to accomplish after that won't ever succeed. It's magick's way of "giving the finger" to them. As an example, here's what happened to my old roommate in LA. She had asked me for help getting a project going, so I had her work a simple ritual to request assistance from a deity for a project. But when a great opportunity suddenly presented itself to her, she denied it was the magick, and with this denial, the opportunity vanished just as quickly as it appeared. Later, she went so far as to blamed the deity for the failure, so all future prospects also disappeared.

My ex manifested $100 using a simple mini-ritual, but she did not acknowledge it was the magick, she assigned simple random luck in finding the $100-dollar note. When she then tried the simple exercise again, it failed and hasn't worked for her since.

If you are working money magick, thank the magick for working if you even find a 10% off coupon. I publicly gave thanks to "The Lady" for winning some money in last night's lottery the very next day. Not a lot, but it was double what I spent, and all due to the magick I have been working.

Track the effects to identify your magick as it starts to operate. Even when it's something as simple as finding a tiny coin or meeting a new acquaintance after using love magick. The acknowledgment doesn't have to be public, but in your mind give send a thanks to the spirit who helped you.

DAVID THOMPSON

CHAPTER TWO

What is Fortune?

The Oxford English Dictionary gives us the standard meaning of the word "Fortune" as chance or luck, especially in the way it affects people's lives.

As used in this book, Fortune means to be "Fortunate in life", be it attracting the perfect mate, the perfect job, discovery of a hidden fortune, or simple living a life of ease and luxury.

The Roman goddess Fortuna is a goddess of luck and fortune. My book on Fortuna has helped thousands of readers in ways that are hard to enumerate. This book intends to expand on this concept, giving the occult practitioner a set of tools and ritual systems to shift chance or luck to favor the magick practitioner. For me, that is the entire purpose of magick — the unlevelling of the playing field to give me the advantage over others.

Fortune is both the pursuit of money, luck, and fame, as well as the end result of these pursuits.

Using Fortune magick isn't cheating.

Gambling and Magick

You have read or heard someone asking that if magick works, why haven't witches won the lottery, or why daemonologists don't win at poker? Skeptics will also point out that psychics haven't won money in Las Vegas, etc, etc, ad nauseam.

In a small book about remote viewing and gambling, the author points out that remote viewers **have won money in the lottery.** They're just not vocal about it. The average human living their life does not know how many practitioners of the occult have successfully won games of chance. That's because we don't go around bragging about our victories.

Personally, I have won e-games in the lotto many times while working out the system in this book. I haven't won huge... Yet. But I have made money. I'll put down $2.00 on the Powerball lottery and win $10.00 on that ticket. I won $25 with a $5.00 e-game scratchoff while testing the gambling sigil. I expect I'll continue exploring this and I won't go around bragging about my winnings. However, if I win the major jackpot, I'll likely disappear and there'll only be the occasional book.

All that being said, I again repeat my disclaimer: *I cannot give any guarantees that this book will assist you in changing your luck with games of chance.*

The magick rituals in this book are designed to shift your

energy to accommodate the energy stream that accompanies luck magick. This magick will slightly nudge the dice to assist you in playing roulette or jiggle the cards to help you win at blackjack, but this magick will not stop you from "pressing your luck" and losing your winnings if the cards or dice begin to turn against you. Play the games responsibly.

In one ritual, I specifically have you ask The Lady or The Seven to help you know when to stop and walk away. There are tales of people winning in casinos who watch their winnings literally pile up, only to lose it all in subsequent games.

Never spend money gambling that needs to be spent elsewhere. Only spend money you can easily lose and not miss. Don't be that person who spends all the vacation cash in the first night at a casino.

CHAPTER THREE

Preparations

Few of us can just decide to work a ritual and head into the altar space, cast a fast circle, and then summon a spirit. You might need a bit of preparation first.

Gather up the gold candles needed for The Lady. Print the sigils. Prepare the ritual candle by anointing it with oils, mix the incense, and obtain the offering.

The biggest part of preparing for a ritual is to craft your petition. In this book, I will give you examples of what to say in the petition, but make sure to word your petition to fit your desire and circumstances.

I have found, through deliberate trial and error (mostly error) that if I write my desire on paper, and continue to ponder the desire, the more focused my ability to drill-down, or to simplify, the desire so that it can be worded into a very simple statement.

Most people, when asked what their desire is, will begin this wandering and elaborate description of what they want, including all the insignificant details and conditions. It's like listening to a child tell a story.

Don't be like that.

Let's dig out the old "headology" books and look past the surface and go deep into the desire.

Often, the desire for a "new house" is rooted in the desire for "security".

A new car might be that your old cars need to be reliable and that feeds into the "security" desire again.

A new life partner = security.

Fifteen million dollars? That's the desire to be a wealthy person and yeah, that's also security, but it also comes with first class air travel, great food and well… Go for it!

I always tell people it takes the same amount of magick to manifest five hundred dollars as it takes to manifest five dollars.

It takes writing this down on paper. Doing the actual work of writing helps begin the magick. I have a special roller-ball pen I use. I've used it to make notes in my journal and drill down to the core of my desire while working up a petition. I've gotten to where I can craft a petition statement quickly, however; I am a writer and I have had to summarize a lengthy novel or screenplay in a single sentence of under twenty-five words, so I got good at this task.

Your task now is to grab a pad of paper and something to write with, and begin writing your desire. Define it. At this point, you may just be drawn to something, so write down all vague feelings.

As you write things down, the law of attraction begins to work.

(Law of Attraction, where one thought leads to another, which leads to a third, all on the same subject, etc.)

After a few minutes, or days, you will have a piece of paper with ideas, desires, scratched out desires and ideas, then more ideas. But eventually, through continuous effort, your petition statement will begin to appear.

Then it's on to writing the actual petition.

Magick Ink and the Petition

Many books will instruct the student to use special inks and papers when writing a petition for a ritual. This book is no different, except I'll pass along to you some nifty tricks to avoid paying money for what is just plain old paper and ink.

Magick ink is only magick because we said it was magick.

I'll use any of the "special pens" I have on hand. That roller-ball pen is one of them. Another is a mid-priced fountain pen with Diamine "Oxblood" ink, both of which I regard as "unique." I took a little bottle of the ink and placed it in my circle with the pen, and I just envisioned energy blasting both items.

Magick ink can also be made with any fountain pen ink and a single drop of blood. I have found that adding blood to fountain pen ink to be effective in turning ink into magick ink. However, it's often too thick then to work in a fountain pen using the ink in the ink system, so I will just dip the pen into the small bottle of ink and write. Just make sure to clean it with water afterwards.

Crafting this magick ink is easy. Find a bottle of some inexpensive ink, such as Waterman, Pelikan, or Parker. Get a small, empty ink bottle with a good cap (a 1/2 ounce, or about 15-30ml, sized bottle with solid caps). Using a diabetic lancet, prick a finger and put a drop of blood into the empty bottle. Then use an eye dropper to fill the bottle about 1/3 to 1/2 full with the ink. Cap the bottle, give it a slight shake, and done! Magick Ink!

Altar Supplies

My altar is kept minimal. I use four basic candles, two white and two black. I have two incense burners, one for stick and one for resin, a pendulum and chart for answers, my notepad or journal.

The rituals in this book will all share the same basic list of supplies. Those supplies are:

Basic altar candles

Incense burner and charcoal

Specific magick oils

Offering bowl and diabetic lancets (for blood offerings)

Special Sigils

Optional items for your altar will vary based upon your own tastes. Items such as crystals, daggers, wands, wine goblets, and more. It all depends on the size of your altar.

Basic Altar Candles

Even a temporary altar will need one or two base candles, plus the specific candle for either The Lady or The Seven. I keep mine simple: two black and two white candles.

For the spirits in this book, you'll need at least two gold candles, preferably something large, so you can use the same candle over and over for each ritual. Make sure you have separate candles! Don't use the same gold candle for The Lady that you use for the Seven daemons.

For my gold candles, I purchased a brand called "Mega Candles" in the 3" by 3" (7.6cm x 7.6cm) round pillar candles.

Ritual candles are separate from the candles for the spirits. I go with the small spell or chime candles. I have a collection of heavy-duty glass candle holders for these. In a grocery store, go into the fragrances and air freshener section. There, you'll most likely find some scented candles. The most common brand is "Glade" (not sure about the rest of the planet, but here in the US) which are in short, thick glasses. After burning these out, cleaning them up and removing stickers, what you have left is a solid candle holder for chime candles. I place a small square of aluminum foil in the bottom, and when the chime candle is burned out, it's easy clean-up.

Candle Preparation

The rituals in this book will need one gold candle for each section: One for The Lady and one for The Seven. I have crafted a simple sigil for each, which you will need to draw on the candles. I use a paint pen, but you can carve them with a push-pin or use a permanent ink marker.

After buying or making oil, the small candle for each ritual is coated in a small amount of an oil as part of the ritual. After oiling up the spell candle, I usually melt the bottom of it and stick it to the foil in the candle holder. Have a small cloth handy to wipe the oil off of your hands.

Annotating the candle is a simple enough process, although some ritual books will make it a detailed process. It's really no big deal. A drop of oil on your left hand, place the candle in your left hand and draw the oil from the top to the bottom.

Incense

Most of the rituals in this book require actual incense. Frankincense is the most recommended and preferred resin to use. It is burned in a small charcoal holder, which is placed on a wooden coaster. The resin is gently dropped onto the burning charcoal, and it begins to smoke.

My other books would recommend to use essential oils if you could not burn real incense. This isn't as good as actual incense, because the burning of frankincense is a way to purify your altar space. Sage doesn't cut it when banishing negative energies. Essential oil diffusers will send out the aroma, but it's not the same effect. Part of each ritual is the representation of the four elements: Earth, Fire, Water, Air. Incense represents Air.

Finding what you need is as easy as going online. Most areas even have local shops where you can get a supply of charcoal and a burner. Most will even have the resins. If not, seek out a resin sampler online. It's what I did, and I haven't run out of the resins after two years. Except frankincense, as I use it every time.

Frankincense is preferred by four out of five daemons when asked. Wait, I understand those four daemons have punished that fifth daemon, so it's now unanimous: Use frankincense.

During the Master Ritual, you will need an incense blend. This is easy to make.

Master Ritual Incense Blend:
- 2 parts frankincense
- 1 part White copal
- 1 part dragon's blood
- Pinch of cinnamon

Crush, but do not powder the incense resins. (I use a small freezer bag, drop some large chunks of the resin into it, and hit it with a hammer on solid ground. Dragon's blood comes in huge chunks, so be ready to do some hammering.)

Measure out the proportions, and put into a small jar, then shake.

For a ritual, I keep a long handled iced tea spoon handy to drop incense on the charcoal.

The Lady's Incense

Incense for The Lady is a bit easier. She is happy with frankincense, or frankincense mixed with small amounts of White copal and sweet myrrh. For Joss Sticks, she loves honeysuckle or patchouli. Morning Star brand patchouli sticks are her favorite. Nag Champa if you can't find any of the others.

Magick Oils

Each ritual will require one or more specific oils. I typically obtain mine online, using the brand "Art of the Root". These are high quality and are effective. I also have recipes for the oils in the appendix.

Use this sparingly, a little goes a long way. A single drop will cover a spell candle. You can also put a drop on the sigil or talisman during the ritual as well.

Offerings

You will need a second copy of the master sigil and a diabetic lancet for the Master Ritual, because when working with The Seven, they will ask for a blood sacrifice. Burnt offerings and eggs are all good to use in simple rituals when working one-on-one with a Daemon, but when calling all these together, you will need to do something special.

For the blood sacrifice, a single drop of blood is sufficient. There is no need to bleed all over the sigil, altar cloth and your clothes when doing this. You will not be killing an innocent (or otherwise) animal, and using its blood. A blood sacrifice is special in that you are giving the daemons a part of yourself.

When it's time for the sacrifice, you will be directed to prick a finger and drop blood onto the small sigil. After a few moments, when the blood has dried a bit, you then touch a corner of the sigil to a candle flame, and burn the paper with your blood. This is why you will need a fire-proof bowl. I use two aluminum pie "tins", one inside the other for heat containment. A heavy ceramic bowl will also work. I will use the long handle spoon to lift the paper to allow it to burn completely.

Other offerings will vary by ritual, but as a general guideline, I will list the acceptable offerings for The Lady below:

Flowers

Fresh fruit

Honey

Cream

Red wine (no other types of wine)

Sweet foods such as cake

Chocolate

She suggests that you also give her offerings after using her magick to win. Mostly flowers placed on her sigil. Place the offering in a small bowl and set it on her master sigil. Allow it to stay at least overnight.

Special Sigils

This book contains a master sigil for The Lady and The Seven, as well as the two genius spirits. You can craft permanent talismans out any of these sigils. A link to an artist who knows how to make these sigils is in the appendix.

I also have a simplified sigil for use on the main gold candles.

Also included are new Power, Fortune and Luck sigils. The sigils are activated and will be useful in any ritual performed from this book, and need to be combined with the sigils for The Lady or The Seven.

Although activated, you will also need to attune these sigils to your own energy. This is a simple process and is done in a very easy ritual.

You will need a single candle and frankincense. Light the candle and charcoal. When the frankincense is smoking well, hold the printed sigil, or permanent talisman, over the incense smoke and visualize your own energy, gold or purple in color, flowing from your hand and into the sigil. Hold this for only a moment. Do this for each sigil you have printed or have had made into a talisman.

With a permanent talisman, you will usually need to activate it once every three to four months.

Keep these with you while buying lotto tickets, seeking your fortune, interviewing, or in a casino.

The Alpha State

Many of these pathworkings require an altered state of mind known as "alpha". This state has many terms, but most are incorrect. It's simply "alpha" and it's a state of relaxation which allows communication with your subconscious mind. There are many levels of alpha, from a light trance state to an almost napping state.

For most of these pathworkings, the light trance is usually all that is needed.

To help you enter the alpha state, you can look for MP3 audios online or search for streaming video sites. I also provide a few meditation audios that cover the initial induction and allow you to enter the deepest alpha and then theta states.

Going into an alpha state is a simple process outside of audios. Did you know that we can already enter alpha and often have no idea this has happened until we suddenly snap back to alertness? Remember zoning out in class while in high school? Driving and suddenly realizing you've driven halfway home without realizing it? The dreamy feeling you get just before waking up, when you can easily recall a dream?

That is alpha.

The trick is to enter into that state on cue. At first, I did not have any audios, so I followed directions in a witchcraft book. I'd sit and just relax. Deep breaths, and then I'd focus on my feet, making them relax. Then my lower legs and then up to my thighs. Then my torso, allowing it to relax, then my hands and arms.

More deep breathing, and more relaxing, up my neck and across my head.

Try this yourself. Put this book down, and focus on breathing, and just allow your body to relax. Pay attention to how this feels. Just relax.

It's okay at this point if you "tune out," which means to fall asleep. Sometimes, if falling asleep keeps being a problem, practice when you have had plenty of sleep, or perhaps take a vitamin E capsule and some honey.

After a few times, you should be able to drop into an alpha state easily. Then you can begin to add counting down to deepen your trance state. Start by just visualizing walking down a short set of stairs. Only five or six stairs at first.

Once at the bottom, take a moment to check yourself, how your body feels in this state. At this time, give yourself a physical cue to drop into alpha. I will place my left thumb between my first and middle finger of my left hand, and press. I'll tell myself that when I do this, while intending to go into alpha, I'm there.

It works.

It works so well, don't even think about testing this while doing something needing your full attention.

The points in each ritual where you stop to meditate and visualize should be done while in alpha, and work the entire pathworking rituals while in alpha. Your success rates will improve almost immediately.

This is because when you visualize in alpha, you are making direct communication with your subconscious, which is the key to making magick work. If your subconscious thinks the desire has already manifested, then it'll unlock the magick and your desire will manifest.

PART TWO

CHAPTER FOUR

The Lady

It's interesting to note that the concept of Fortune and Luck seems to always be associated with the feminine. "Lady Luck". Goddesses in multiple pantheons are associated with luck, and various rituals and prayers to these divine beings can be found spread across history. Somewhere, even now, someone is sending up a silent prayer to "Lady Luck" as they insert money into a gambling machine, or toss a pair of dice across a craps table.

Just who is this elusive "Lady Luck" spirit? Yes, there is an actual being that I consider to be "The Lady". She's not Fortuna, although they share some similarities, but there is an actual Goddess of Luck. She is a collection of various gambling and luck deities from many religions and magical practices. She is known by multiple names throughout history.

How did I come to find out about this elusive goddess?

I was doing some astral traveling, and I went into a small work area I had created years ago, using a guided meditation. (See appendix for leads to finding these). While there, I am often met by a guide or a being I regularly work with. This time, it was Fortuna. I took a moment to thank her for her graces in this book series, and I saw there was another feminine spirit in the background. Fortune said a goddess wished to meet with me. This goddess stepped forward, and I clearly saw her for the first time. She projected her name, but not only was it incomprehensible to a human, I have now forgotten it. She then said to just call her "The Lady", which reminded me of a character in a fantasy novel I'd read years ago.

She was tall and emitted a golden light. To say she was beautiful is to stretch that word beyond its earthly meaning. Think of Aphrodite, Helen of Troy, Hera, and even Lilith's beauty. Then add on a few levels, and you will have The Lady.

She possesses a soothing, calm energy. She is seen with golden skin tones, wearing golden robes, and a bright golden glow all around.

This golden glow is also a healing glow, and it also transforms negative energy. In this, she is a most useful goddess to have around, so if your space is steeped in horrid negative energy because of roommates, neighbors, family members, then her energy can blast all that away and transform the people causing it.

Approaches Using Rituals

The lady is a rather elusive spirit, but she will show up when summoned using this method. There is also an accompanying pathworking, but I advise that you use this ritual prior to doing the simpler rituals.

Each ritual will be as simple as possible, given the type of goddess energy you are asking to join you. The Lady is on that vague, foggy, wobbly line between "Goddess" and "Daemoness" where many feminine beings seem to exist.

As with any other goddess, one must be respectful and polite, and at no time assume The Lady is going to accept your petition. It's important that gratitude rituals with offerings are done after each success. It's really important to The Lady that we show proper gratitude.

But don't overdo it.

By that, I mean there is no reason to ingratiate yourself with The Lady, by piling dozens of flowers on an altar dedicated to her, or to pile fruit and bread daily on a space dedicated to her. A simple arrangement of flowers or a single glass of good wine placed on her symbol for twenty-four hours is sufficient. I have seen altars dedicated to goddesses go well over the "ingratiating" threshold. One photo I saw had so many flowers that the altar wasn't even visible.

Don't do that.

During a ritual, you may get indications a specific desire can't occur. As you work with The Lady, you might be able to get immediate feedback on a petition. This might be simply a feeling she said "No", or it can happen later when you suddenly lose money while at a casino.

When this happens, you need to step back and see if you worked the ritual correctly, if you had set reasonable goals for the manifestation. With a lottery ritual sequence, begin small. Then work up. Small wins with scratch-off tickets, $10 and $50 dollar wins with a lottery drawing. You might experience a series of losses; at which time it'd be wise to go into ritual and ask if The Lady can indicate why she might have stopped helping you.

On these occasions, you might need to turn to divination, doing a tarot card reading or using a pendulum, to ascertain the answer to what might be happening.

In most cases, it's because you had set your expectations too high, wanting to manifest a huge jackpot win versus a series of smaller wins.

The sequence I have you work will allow the energy to build and after several rituals, the magick will really take hold and begin to deliver results that will be well beyond your expectations.

Approaches using Pathworking

I play fast and loose with the term "pathworking".

Most traditional magicians define pathworking as mentally projecting up and around the paths of the Kabalistic Tree of Life in order to gain information, instructions, meet entities there, and ask favors of those entities. Recently, magicians and teachers (like myself) have shifted the term to mean a series of visualizations to attune yourself to the energies of specific beings and allow direct contact, to allow you to quickly state a petition and manifest using the beings' energy.

When it comes to pathworking The Lady, it is necessary to run a standard ritual to her prior to doing a pathworking. The pathworking method is perfect for those times when you are in a casino or other place of legal ([1]) gambling and can't really haul out the gold candle and incense, much less do any circle casting. For example, you can duck into the restrooms and close yourself in a private stall, quickly center yourself and ask The Lady to lend a hand with your efforts. Just make sure that you are alone when you speak, or pretend you are on a phone call. Or say the words in your head, The Lady will hear you.

---

[1] You ARE gambling in a legal environment, right? Because this is ONLY for LEGAL gambling. (wink)

CHAPTER FIVE

Basic Ritual to The Lady

Like most of the goddess and daemons I have written about, there is a basic ritual to be done to contact The Lady.

Depending on the specific ritual, you will also need the basics, such as altar candles, and a dedicated Goddess Candle. So, here's a list of the basic items needed for a full-up High Magick ritual to this elusive goddess.

Altar Items:

- Altar Candles. (I usually use one black and one white, but you can use any neutral color, with white being preferred.)
- Goddess Sigil, printed or have it made into an altarpiece.
- Ritual specific sigil.

- Goddess Candle: Gold. Go with a large pillar candle in gold. Draw her Candle Sigil on the side.
- Ritual candle: Usually a small gold candle. You can use silver as well.
- Incense: Resins, go with Frankincense, benzoin, myrrh, white copal. Flower blooms work as well. Cinnamon is also good for mixing into this.
- Incense sticks: Honeysuckle, Vanilla Flower, Lavender are preferred. Patchouli incense from Morning Star is her favorite.
  - (*If you cannot burn incense, you can attempt to use essential oils. This is one time when you really, really need to use incense to make the Goddess feel as if you really want her help. She may not help if you skip the incense.)
- Offerings. She has requested flowers, red wine, fresh fruit, sweet bread (cake) or a special and expensive incense such as Agarwood (also known as Oud or Aloeswood) or Mayan Copal.
- Colors: **GOLD**. Gold designs on the altar cloth, gold-colored offering bowls, or bright brass, Gold foil, Fortune oil with tiny gold flakes in it. "King Midas" oil, "Fast Luck Oil", and similar. All found online, see the Appendix.

Specific rituals will also have additional items, such as lottery play slips, casino chips, playing cards.

The basic ritual is as follows:

You begin by lighting the incense and candles, then turn off the room lights.

Cast a basic circle (see Appendix).

Then call to The Lady:

Goddess of timeless Beauty, gold is thy light.

Goddess of fortune, gambling and wagering,

Goddess of wealth, of power, and of influence.

Goddess, there are those who see you as fickle, as mercurial, and elusive.

I ask now that you join with me to prove them wrong.

I ask that you be at my side, to guide me,

I ask that you whisper into my ear

When to play and when to depart.

I ask that you cover me in your golden aura

Surround me in gold

Imbue my energy with the energy of fortune

Flood my aura with the energy of wealth

Allowing all my wagers to win.

I now ask that: (your petition)

After reading your petition, stop a moment and fully visualize the results occurring. Go into detail, fully live the magick manifesting.

Once you have stated your petition, then it's time for the candle and talisman.

Hold your hands around the candle, at about an inch away. Then say:

Goddess! I now ask that you enchant this candle to bring to me (your request).

Visualize golden energy blasting into the candle. Starting at the top, slowly bring your hands down to the altar. Energizing is now completed.

Hold your hands out and over the sigil or talisman. Say:

Goddess, I now ask that you enchant this (sigil/talisman) **to assist me in** (your request).

Visualize a swirling vortex of gold and silver energy surrounding the sigil/talisman. Allow this to continue for at least twenty breaths.

Pick up the offering and place it in the bowl, and set it on The Lady's sigil. Then say: **Goddess, my gratitude for your assistance knows no bounds, and I ask that you please accept this humble offering as a symbol of my gratitude.**

To close the ritual, say: **This ritual is now complete. Goddess, I ask that you be with me while I play** (your game or lottery). **Be with me and guide me.**

CHAPTER SIX

Approaches Using Pathworking/Meditation

Pathworking The Lady is best done only after working the full ritual. This way, a relationship is established and she'll be more willing to arrive and bless your talisman or candle.

After the pathworking, and especially after any wins, leave an offering for her on your altar, or if you don't have a full-time altar, then pick some place special where you can have her sigil and then place the offering on it.

A Path to Fortune

Pathworking is a mental only ritual, and can be performed in most places as long as you have a moment of peace and quiet. As with the standard ritual, make sure you have a statement of desire in your mind, or written on a small piece of paper, and have a small offering as well, unless out in public (next section).

This pathworking is designed to bring you "general" fortune. I'll cover more specific gambling or winning pathworking in the next chapter. Your desire should be something like, "Assist me in winning in this job interview." "Assist me in convincing my boss that I deserve the raise." "Lend me your assistance in getting my beloved to say yes to marriage."

You could ask for help in landing a new contract. Buying a house or new car, pretty much anything as long as the intended results will not harm or otherwise injure someone else.

This is, literally, a path to the near astral plane, and the symbology sends your focus to the area where The Lady typically resides. This is her home, essentially, so politely approach her and take care to mind your manners.

The visuals:

A misty gray darkness.

Looking down, you see a well-worn dirt path. You begin walking.

In the distance is an orb. It's a dull silver color.

As you get closer, the orb grows in brightness.

The path leads into the orb, so you step through.

The other side is bright, with gold buildings in the distance.

The Lady awaits you by a small fountain with flowing liquid gold.

Greet her and ask her to grant you favor. If you have a prepared statement, read it now. Wait for her reaction. She will either smile and nod, or shake her head "no" and perhaps place her finger over her lips.

If she says "Yes" by nodding, thank her by projecting gratitude towards her, usually a bright pink energy. Smile and turn, walking back out of the portal and into the mist.

If she denies your petition, you may ask her why. Be prepared to accept her reason. At this point, depart by walking away, back to the portal and into the mist. Take a minute to examine the reason she may have turned you down. There could be many reasons, so take this into account if you decide to ask again, and rephrase your request to one where she'll gladly lend her energy to manifest your desire.

Perhaps you ask that an offer on a house be accepted, but there is another family who would be a better "fit" for the house, or you are asking to marry someone whose karma isn't to be your life partner.

In these cases, don't press by asking again, simply take her "no" as final and then do some divination to determine what is the next course of action. Maybe there is some future event she knows of that will adversely affect your life if you were to buy that house, or the new car payments will be beyond your means.

When she says yes to assisting you, plan to give her an offering once you have returned to waking consciousness. As discussed in the standard ritual, allow the offering to stay on her sigil for at least overnight. Then take it outside and dispose of it into nature.

Pathworking in Public

There's a great number of things that really shouldn't be performed in public, and a full magick ritual is one of them. I'd imagine the staff and security in a casino would frown upon your unfolding a gold altar cloth, setting up with candles and incense next to the blackjack tables. You might even be asked to leave. They might not even be polite about asking you to depart.

The standard pathworking needs a distraction free environment, and a written petition, plus the offering for her altar. But perhaps you are suddenly given the opportunity to get a second interview for that fantastic job while you are wrapping up the initial interview. Perhaps you are on a road trip and decide at the last minute to stop at a casino for a few games, or stop in a store and grab a lottery ticket.

In a work environment, your best bet would be to excuse yourself and visit the bathroom. If there isn't anyone else in the facilities, you can work this standing at the mirror. Look at yourself and close your eyes. Count yourself into the alpha state quickly. Visualize the following:

> **Yourself in the mirror.**
> **A silver orb appears behind you in the mirror.**
> **The Lady steps out and is behind you in the mirror.**
> **Look her in the eyes and mentally ask her for help.**
> **She'll nod and smile.**

Open your eyes and then take a deep breath.

Remember to leave her an offering when you finish the interview and return home.

Variations on this scenario can be while stopped outside a store and you feel the urge to buy a lottery ticket. Turn the rear-view mirror so that you see yourself, or drop the sun visor if it has a mirror. Visualize:

Yourself in the mirror.

The Lady appears behind you in your car.

Perhaps she leans forward so that she is directly behind you.

Make eye contact and ask her to bless you buying a lottery ticket.

Watch for her reaction.

If she says no, thank her anyway and then decide if you really want to buy that lottery ticket right now, or wait until she says yes. She is used to people going ahead and gambling when she says she will not help. I've done that myself. Then I've lost the money and I have only myself to blame.

CHAPTER SEVEN

Rituals for Mindset Shift

This is a series of rituals designed to take you from a specific mindset where you seem to be having "bad" luck and flip that around so that you have "good" luck, or at least better luck than before.

Unlike other desires, and unlike other books on magick, in this chapter I will encourage you to work these rituals multiple times.

Most are quite simple, only requiring a few items from the standard ritual.

This sequence is designed to purge "loser thoughts" using The Lady (versus Marbas, the daemon used in Part Two's block removals), and this is a ritual which can be reworked at any time you experience a loss, and feel as if your luck might have shifted.

Bad Luck Purge

Like the ritual in part two, this ritual will work to purge "bad luck" thought forms from your mind.

This cartoon of a broken mirror is in the downloads found in the link in the appendix. Download and print it out.

After printing the image, it's time for a short ritual.

This small ritual will need a candle or two, a red marker, and a fireproof bowl.

With only candles lit, look at the cartoon, then using a red marker, draw a RED slash through it.

On the back, write "I banish thee!" with the marker.

Stare at the drawing, then touch the paper to a candle and shout at the image "I banish THEE!" while it burns.

Once it has been reduced to ashes, spit onto the ashes three times.

Once this is done, take the bowl outside and dump the ashes onto the ground, grinding the ashes into the earth with your foot. I mean, really GRIND the ashes. Banish those thoughts!

The ritual is done!

Accepting Good Luck

Does it appear to you it's always other those people who are fortunate? That they're more fortunate that you?

This might not be an actual problem for you. But I advise you run this short exercise before the rest of The Lady winning sequence, as you just might have a small bit of resistance hiding inside your subconscious somewhere.

It's easy to recognize this in other people. People who can't seem to accept gifts, who always downplay their stroke of good luck, brushing it off as chance. Develop a since of "Yeah, of course I had good luck! Doesn't everyone?"

This exercise is used to uncover that hidden mindset and bring it to the surface so you can deal with it.

Step One:

Grab a sheet of paper. At the top, write down "LUCK" or "FORTUNE" or 'WINNING".

Just below that, write down your first thoughts when you think of other people having streaks of great luck and winning.

Are there any hints of jealousy in there? Just lurking below the surface? Write that down.

Write down all your thoughts surrounding other people being

lucky.

Jealous thoughts are often accompanied by the idea that luck belongs to other people.

Keep writing.

Don't rush this. Put the paper down after thirty minutes and go do something else. Later that day, go back to this exercise. Continue coming up with words that you associate with the term "Luck".

After you have a list, sit back and look at the words you have. What are those words? What feelings are associated with those words?

Step Two:

Grab a thesaurus and look up the antonyms of those words.

A word like "Jealous" has an antonym like "supportive". "Frustrated" is "uplifted".

"Disappointed" is "heartened".

So, now cross out the negative words. Focus on the positive words.

Look at a fortunate person, someone who's won a lottery jackpot, and make yourself feel happy for that person.

There are two things to do at this point.

One: Burn the paper with the negative words, followed by a short ritual to The Lady, asking her to fill your heart with acceptance, allowing luck to enter your subconscious.

Two: grab some guided meditations designed to combat this. I can suggest one right away, *"The Awesome Power of Luck" by Dick Sutphen,* which can be found on Spotify and a few other streaming services. See the Appendix.

On the Go Winning

I've simplified this ritual so that it can be worked without a lot of preparation, as long as you already have the ritual items handy: A single gold candle, two copies of The Lady's sigil (or sigil and talisman), a simple offering, casino chips or other prop, the Fortune Oil, essential oils (pick one: cinnamon, lavender, or lemon), a gold or green cloth or scarf, and about ten minutes.

Perfect offerings for this are flowers, as you can lay them out in the bathroom and, usually, no one will bother it, especially if looks like you're setting out an arrangement. You can even guy a special vase, and draw her sigil on the vase. No one would notice.

This one is more effective than a pathworking ritual, as it's a bit more involved and that tends to draw in your real source of power, the subconscious, into the process and makes the magick work better.

I have designed this fast ritual so it can be worked in a hotel room, or in a guest room. Thus, no incense.

Note: Do work this after a standard ritual to The Lady. So that you have already established a relationship, and it's not just some random person summoning her to a hotel room in Las Vegas. She reacts poorly to that.

Quickly and quietly gather up the items needed, and spread them out on a small table or bathroom counter. Light the candle. Put a small amount of essential oil out in a diffuser or on a cotton ball, to help create the mood. Place the talisman or sigil in the center, then the short prayer to The Lady, followed by your desire.

Word your petition as simply as possible. I've used such phrases as "Lady, please enchant this talisman to bind me to your fortune and luck, allowing me to win and win big."

When ready, shut off the lights.
Say:
Goddess of timeless Beauty, gold is thy light.
Goddess of fortune, gambling and wagering,
Goddess of wealth, of power, and of influence.
I ask that you be at my side, to guide me,
I ask that you cover me in your golden aura
Surround me in gold
Imbue my energy with the energy of fortune
Flood my aura with the energy of wealth
Allowing all my wagers to win.
I now ask that: (your petition)

After reading your petition, pick up the talisman or sigil, and put a small drop of the Fortune Oil on it, and hold it over The Lady's sigil. Visualize golden light surrounding your hand and the talisman/sigil. See this light now spreading to cover you and the entire room.

Pause a moment, and take a deep breath. Visualize WINNING. See the actual situation in the casino or in the line to buy a lottery ticket. Go into detail! Playing the game(s) you wish to play, and see the money, or stack of chips, being given over to you.

Another deep breath, then pick up the offering, placing it on her sigil.

Lady, please accept this humble offering of _____ in return for your patronage. Please accompany me while I go win some games!

At this point, the ritual is over. Lights back on, snuff out the candle, and proceed to play your game.

This, or a revised form of this ritual, can be worked every day while you are visiting a casino, or just before going out to a store to play the lottery.

CHAPTER EIGHT

Advantages over Rivals

It doesn't matter if the person is a business rival, or a rival for someone's affections, you can ask "The Lady" for assistance in changing the dynamics of the situation to give you an advantage over this other person or business.

For this ritual, you will need to know who you need to beat. It could be another business or a person in the company that is a rival for a new position or for an award. No matter the situation, you need to project the energy of success, of being better than the other party, so that the people making the decision will see you in a more favorable light.

Business Advantage Ritual

It doesn't matter what you are up against, this ritual will give you an advantage. Adjust the sample petition to match your situation. The ritual is almost the same as the basic ritual, with the difference being that you are asking The Lady to surround you with an energy of power, fortune, and charisma, which will give you (or your business) the advantage over other businesses or individuals.

Word your petition somewhat like this, adjusted to fit your situation:

Goddess of Luck! I ask that you surround me with the energy of power, power over my rivals, giving me the advantage. I project this power and charisma, it floods all around me, giving me/my business advantages over _____!

Altar Items:

- Altar Candles.
- Goddess Sigil
- Power Sigil
- Gold goddess candle
- Red "power" spell candle
- "Crown of Success" oil
- Incense: Frankincense, benzoin, cinnamon powder
- Offering and offering bowl
- Rival's business name or person's name, business card or flier.

The ritual:

You begin by lighting the incense and candles, then turn off the room lights.

Cast a basic circle.

Then call to The Lady:

Goddess of timeless Beauty, gold is thy light.

Goddess of fortune, gambling and wagering,

Goddess of wealth, of power, and of influence.

Goddess, there are those who see you as fickle, as mercurial, and elusive.

I ask now that you join with me to prove them wrong.

I ask that you be at my side, to guide me,

I ask that you cover me in your golden aura

Surround me in gold

Imbue my energy with the energy of charisma

Flood my aura with the energy of power

Giving me advantage over all others

Now read your petition.

After reading your petition, stop a moment and fully visualize the results occurring. Go into detail, fully live the magick manifesting. Pick up the rival's business card or paper with their name. Imagine you/your business next to this other person/business. Imagine that you suddenly glowing, growing taller, standing out from the others. Hold this for at least 20 breaths.

Once you have finished your visualizations, then it's time for the candle and talisman.

Hold your hands around the candle, about an inch away. Then say:

Goddess! I now ask that you enchant this candle to cover me with your power and charisma!

Visualize golden-red energy blasting into the candle. Starting at the top, slowly bring your hands down to the altar. Energizing is now completed.

Hold your hands out and over the sigil or talisman. Say:

Goddess, I now ask that you enchant this (sigil/talisman) **to give me advantages over my business rivals/personal rivals. I rise to the top!**

Visualize a swirling vortex of gold and silver energy surrounding the sigil/talisman. Allow this to continue for at least twenty breaths.

Pick up your offering and place it in the bowl, and set it on The Lady's sigil. Then say: **Goddess, my gratitude for your assistance knows no bounds, and I ask that you please accept this humble offering as a symbol of my gratitude.**

To close the ritual, say: **This ritual is now complete. Goddess, I ask that you be with me while I go about my business. Be with me and guide me.**

Advantage Over Love Rival Ritual

Love magick is a bit out of the usual repertoire for The Lady, yet by projecting charisma and power, you can gain advantages over another by - literally - creating a glow around you that attracts the other person's attention. You can use this to JUST gain attention, or you can use this to make yourself stand out among others when your hopeful life partner is surrounded by others wanting the same thing.

Word your petition somewhat like this, adjusted to fit your situation:

Goddess of Luck! I ask that you surround me with the energy of power and charisma, giving me the advantage. I project this power and charisma, it floods all around me, giving me advantages over _____ (or all the others)!

Altar Items:

- Altar Candles.
- Goddess Sigil
- Power Sigil
- Gold goddess candle
- Pink spell candle
- "Come to Me Oil" oil
- Incense: Frankincense, benzoin, cinnamon powder
- Offering and offering bowl
- Rival's name, sample of writing or photograph

The ritual:

You begin by lighting the incense and candles, then turn off the room lights.

Cast a basic circle.

Then call to The Lady:

Goddess of timeless Beauty, gold is thy light.

Goddess of fortune, gambling and wagering,

Goddess of wealth, of power, and of influence.

Goddess, there are those who see you as fickle, as mercurial, and elusive.

I ask now that you join with me to prove them wrong.

I ask that you be at my side, to guide me,

I ask that you cover me in your golden aura

Surround me in gold

Imbue my energy with the energy of charisma

Flood my aura with the energy of power

Giving me advantage over all others

Now read your petition.

After reading your petition, stop a moment and fully visualize the results occurring. Go into detail, fully see the magick manifesting.

Once you have stated your petition, then it's time for the candle and talisman.

Hold your hands around the candle, at about an inch away. Then say:

Goddess! I now ask that you enchant this candle to cover me with your power and charisma!

Visualize golden-red energy blasting into the candle. Starting at the top, slowly bring your hands down to the altar. Energizing is now completed.

Hold your hands out and over the sigil or talisman. Say:

Goddess, I now ask that you enchant this (sigil/talisman) **to give me advantages over my rivals, allowing me to project power and charisma! I attract _____'s (the intended person's name) attention, and he/she sees me in a favorable light!**

Visualize a swirling vortex of gold and silver energy surrounding the sigil/talisman. Allow this to continue for at least twenty breaths.

Pick up the offering and place it in the bowl, and set it on The Lady's sigil. Then say: **Goddess, my gratitude for your assistance knows no bounds, and I ask that you please accept this humble offering as a symbol of my gratitude.**

To close the ritual, say: **This ritual is now complete. Goddess, I ask that you be with me while I am around my intended. Be with me and guide me.**

CHAPTER NINE

Pacts

Practitioners who are a bit more experienced might be asking right now: "Can I do a pact with The Lady?" and the answer is yes, most definitely.

A pact differs from a regular ritual in that this is for a long-term goal, such as a political career, with the end result being elected Governor or Senator, or even further. An actor might wish to enter into a pact so that their life is unusually lucky and advances with great strides, such as award wins and box office success.

For those who might not know, or who might only associate pacts with daemons, you can work a pact with most any spirit you'd summon for a ritual. A pact dispenses with the need to work multiple rituals over the same desire. The question you need to ask yourself is this: "Is my long-term desire in alignment with the goddess I wish to enter into a pact with?"

One potential pact with The Lady would be your career, and being fortunate in your chosen career and seeing continued success.

A pact is quite simple to set up and write. First, define your long-term goal. For example, it might be to own and run a large service business. So, go back to the first steps in this part of this book, and begin defining your long-term goal.

Make sure to take your time on this. There is no need to rush, because then you'll need to revise or even terminate the original pact for a new pact.

A pact is usually written out in Magick Ink, and is later signed with this same ink, but in the ritual. So, make sure to have a pen and the ink with you.

A Pact with The Lady

A good pact is a contract, and it should be written like a regular contract. You address The Lady, say who you are, and that you wish to enter into a contract. The Lady will assist you with manifesting the desire, and you will perform some act of gratitude.

Here's a template you can use for this pact:

Dear Lady!

I, _____, do hereby ask to enter into a pact with you. I ask that you assist me in the manifestation of my innermost desire, namely: (spell out your desire, in detail).

In return, I shall (go into detail. Suggest such things as weekly offerings, public acknowledgment of The Lady's help, performing charitable acts in her name, etc.).

This pact will be in effect until my desire manifests.

On this date, a pact is sealed: (date)

Signed: (your signature)

Pretty simple. Public acknowledgment is tricky. It's best to post on social media, in a group or subreddit, where such posts are allowed. Also, be advised you will attract attention and people will ask questions. However, do not share any rituals from this book, as they are only for the purchasers of this book.

There has been some discussion on what to do with the pact itself. Should it be burned to "activate" the pact? Or just put away someplace special? Personally, I figure the way to end a pact is by burning it, so... Wait to burn it.

Altar Items:

- Altar Candles
- Goddess Candle
- Ritual candle
- Incense
- Goddess Sigil
- The pact ready to sign
- Magick ink and Pen
- Offerings

The pact ritual is as follows:

You begin by lighting the incense and candles, then turn off the room lights.

Cast a basic circle

Then call to The Lady:

Goddess of timeless Beauty, gold is thy light.

Goddess of fortune, gambling and wagering,

Goddess of wealth, of power, and of influence.

Goddess, there are those who see you as fickle, as mercurial, and elusive.

I ask that you be at my side,

I ask that you allow us to enter into a pact!

(Read your pact out loud)

Hold your hands over the pact statement, at about an inch away. Then say:

Goddess! I now ask that we seal this pact!

Visualize golden energy blasting into the pacts. Hold this until it glows with golden energy. Allow this to continue for at least twenty breaths.

Sign the pact at this time, the say:

With my signature, this pact is sealed!

Pick up your offering and place it in the bowl, and set it on The Lady's sigil. Then say: **Goddess, my gratitude for your** assistance knows no bounds, and I ask that you please accept this humble offering as a symbol of my gratitude.

To close the ritual, say: **This ritual is now complete.**

Weekly Pact Offering

Simple and easy. Pick a spot and set The Lady's sigil and her candle down, making sure no one will bother it.

If using flowers, buy a small vase and draw her sigil on it, so that it can be placed anywhere in your home.

Once a week, light a candle, and briefly call on The Lady.

Goddess of timeless Beauty, gold is thy light.

Goddess of fortune, gambling and wagering,

Goddess of wealth, of power, and of influence.

Goddess, there are those who see you as fickle, as mercurial, and elusive.

I ask that you be at my side,

I ask you to accept this humble offering in exchange for her magick in making our pact a reality!

Place the offering on her sigil, and close your eyes. Visualize the Lady arriving and smiling.

This ritual is complete. Extinguish the candle, and allow the offering to stay in place for 24 hrs., then place it outside. Unless you are burning special incense as offering, then monitor the incense until it's burned out.

Ending the Pact

Once a goal has been attained, it's time to end the pact.

Set up a simple ritual in your space, incense, offering, and a candle, plus a fireproof bowl and the pact itself.

Call on The Lady.

Goddess of timeless Beauty, gold is thy light.

Goddess of fortune, gambling and wagering,

Goddess of wealth, of power, and of influence.

Goddess, there are those who see you as fickle, as mercurial, and elusive.

I ask that you be at my side,

I wish to thank you for manifesting my goals, and for working this pact with me.

It is now time to end this pact.

Pick up the pact, and touch the paper to a candle flame. As it burns, put it in the fireproof bowl, and make sure it burns completely.

Now say:

Our goals have been met; thus, our pact is now dissolved. Again, I thank you for assisting me in this goal. As a final gesture of gratitude, I hereby offer to you this humble _____.

Place the offering in the bowl and put the bowl on her sigil.

To end the ritual, say:

Goddess! This ritual is now complete. You may depart, and

please come again when I next call!

Allow the offering to stay on her sigil until the next day, then discard.

PART THREE

CHAPTER TEN

Daemonic Fortune Magick

In this part, we will be working with a group of daemons who have been asked to assist in this book, a group I call "The Seven". I will go over each one in the next section.

The whole idea behind Fortune Magick is to tilt the odds in your favor. No matter how you play the game, the "house" always wins in the end. Otherwise, why would anyone ever go through the expensive process of starting a casino?

As I had covered in the introduction, some people are convinced you can't use magick to win. But I am here to say that yes, you can. No one will eject you from a casino for using magick, unless you show up in black robes and begin saying daemonic ENNs, at which time they'll probably escort you to the front door. So, try to blend in. Wear the Master Sigil on a chain, and perhaps someone might ask about it, but just say it's a "good luck charm", and leave it at that. Be careful, don't go around telling people you used daemonic magick to win at gambling. At the very least, their disbelief might cause the magick to stop working, and in the worst case, the casino owners (if Native American) might even place magick fields around the place to prevent all magick from working. Their magick is seriously powerful.

I've encountered Native American magick several times, the first time in 2001, when I did a road trip to the Grand Canyon. Along the way, we stopped at a roadside tent to pick up some "quaint local native trinkets". As I walked into the tent, I was hit by a dizzy spell. I felt the magick the old guy in the tent had put up. I shook my head and asked if I could sit down. I sat next to the old guy and he smiled at me. "You feel the magick?" he asked. "Yes, I do," I replied. "It's to keep people from stealing," he grinned.

So, do not for a moment think the Native American casinos don't use magick to prevent other magick from working. Count on this, and go in knowing your magick is stronger.

The Seven Daemons of Fortune

In this section of the book, we'll be working with seven daemonic beings who will be summoned for the Master Ritual. I'll simply call them "The Seven" from now on, unless there is a specific spirit used for a specific task. For example, we'll call on Marbas to remove any outside blockages, but we'll call on Bael for any internal blockages, as Marbas tends to work rather roughly.

After introducing you to The Seven, I'll also cover two so-called "genius spirits" who can be used for miscellaneous fortune and gambling magick while you work on the Master Ritual sequence.

Summoning the Seven will take calling on each one, uttering their ENN, until you have summoned each daemon. This usually only takes one summoning statement, rarely more than three.

The daemons we'll be using are:

Bael

Agares

Marbas

Bune

Belphegore

Mammon

Lucifuge

All have complementing powers when it comes to the building of a fortune or for gambling.

The Daemonic Spokesman

Of the seven, during the preparation ritual, one will step forward to act as the interface for the other six daemons. In the initial rituals I did while writing this book, Duke Bune stepped forward as the spokesman for the group while I wrote this book. Bune may not always step forward, as one other may feel their energy is a better match for you.

Later on, in the Master Ritual pathworking, it is this daemon who will be summoned using the Fortune Pathworking. The others may also show up, especially if they carry messages about your magick and manifestation efforts.

Don't expect to have to call one forward. Imagine you have gathered together a group of, say, cats and one will often come forward for head-scratches before the rest will follow along. I mean, you **can ask.** Just don't expect Duke Bune or President Marbas to actually step forward when Mammon might be the better match.

During the preliminary rituals to the Master Ritual, expect one of the Seven to step forward.

The Daemons

I'll go over each daemon and explain why they're a perfect fit for this type of magick, even if other sources don't list fortune and money luck as a primary power. The primary powers of many beings are passed down from occultist to occultist, via grimoires and other writings. One magician might have only used Bael for a single purpose, and his diary reflected this, and the next person didn't bother to look at Bael for anything else. This happens all the time! For example, a particular actor will get "type-cast" as a specific character, and just can't get any other types of acting jobs. Happens with everyone. Another example, a personal one, is that I was assumed to only be a photographer, even by my closest friends, even my ex-wife saw me only as a only photographer, not as a writer or film maker.

My experiences with all spirits, be they gods or daemons is they have a vast array of powers, if we simply just ask them.

So why these seven daemons? During the writing of one of my classes, I went into ritual and asked each being if they're comfortable being in a class about the accumulation of wealth. Prior to this book, I asked the same group if they're on-board with this book's premise. All but one said yes, that they agreed to be a part of this book.

I'll briefly cover what my personal experiences have been with each daemon, and a small bit about what traditional sources might have to say about that spirit. Most commonly used text source is the *"Lemegeton Clavicula Salomonis, or, The little Key of Solomon"*. For this book, I'll refer to this as *The Goetia*. The sources for this text appear to be taken from the *Pseudomonarchia Daemonum*, a text written in 1577 by Johann Weyer.

So, let's take a brief look at each one, and then move on.

King Bael

Bael is also referred to as Ba'al, with his listing in the Goetia as number one. Some practitioners use him as guardian of the east. I use Lucifer, "Morning Star" for the east, but that's up to you. He is quick to arrive when I ask him to join with me, using his common ENN, which is part of the master summoning ritual. Among his more common abilities are to assist the petitioner with being popular, but as a subordinate of Lucifuge Refocal (treasurer of the Underworld) he's often summoned on matters relating to money and wealth. He is the first daemon we will summon in the main ritual. He tends to keep himself at the right edge of my space, but will step forward when addressed. Works well, and prefers a blood sacrifice over anything else.

Duke Agares

Agares is listed second in the Goetia and is given the title of Duke. He is also a subordinate of Lucifuge Rofocale, so he's perfect for money magick. I typically summon him by speaking his ENN three times, but his energy typically arrives within moments of speaking the ENN once. I have only worked with him a few times prior to including him in the original Daemonic Money class. He's a traditionalist, like Bael, and prefers frankincense and a blood sacrifice.

President Marbas

Marbas is listed as a President, and is number five in the Goetia. I first encountered Marbas while doing some work to defeat someone aiming harmful energy at a friend. In one book, he is used to remove the power of an enemy, although the traditional texts have him being one to heal diseases, and literally teach the practitioner. I will say he's quite effective when dealing with people throwing curses everywhere. He's the focus of a chapter in my *Daemons of High Magick* book *(High Magick Book 2)* as well as Chapter 12 of my *Daemons and the Law of Attraction* book *(High Magick Book 3),* so I'd have to say that, aside from Bune and Lilith, he is the daemon I've worked with the most in the past decade. His energy is powerful, and I know when he arrives, as he'll make the incense smoke move and change shape, like Lilith and Apollo. For this book, he'll be used to remove roadblocks and persons who may be blocking your path.

Duke Bune

The 26th spirit of the Goetia, given the title of Duke. He is the first daemon I ever summoned, and I have worked with him extensively in the past ten years. I have covered Bune in many of my other High Magick books, along with my experiences with him. I will add to those books that Bune has now appeared in incense smoke, his goatee quite visible. To me, he appears as a military man, in a green tunic and with greenish hair, which is the description I gave him in one of my fiction novels. His ability to bring one money has made him known as the "ATM" of the Goetia, and is one of the most called upon spirits in the Goetia as a result. He and I are quite connected, so for me, he'll arrive in the temple space prior to the ritual. He's another spirit who prefers a blood sacrifice, but will also accept spirits, such as whiskey or vodka. A good brand, not some cheap swill from the bargain bin. Spend some money, as it's seen as a sacrifice to pour a libation of expensive liquor to Bune.

Belphegore

Not a daemon of the Goetia, Belphegore is commonly seen as a "Fallen" angelic, which places him with Lucifer and is one of the seven princes, or great kings, of hell - which depends on who you're reading, and makes an appearance in quite a few novels and movies/TV shows. Because he is associated with laziness, he will assist in bringing to you your desire in a way that is easy to accomplish. Laziness is seen as a sin, but making life easier is the whole goal of magick. As a fallen angelic, he joins with the likes of many, many powerful spirits, which include one of my own spirit guides, Daniel.

Mammon

Another non-Goetic spirit who is literally the daemon of money. I have worked with him for quite some time, as I enlisted his aid in putting together my Daemonic Money Magick course. No nonsense. He gets to work quickly and will communicate quickly if you are using a pendulum in the ritual. (I cover the use of a pendulum in the pre-ritual.)

Lucifuge

Also known as Lucifuge Refocal, a spirit who's listed in the text, *The Grand Grimoire* as Prime Minister. *The Grand Grimoire* is attributed to one "Alibeck the Egyptian" of Memphis, who purportedly wrote this book in 1517, and lists nine daemons of note, including Lucifer. I have also been working with Lucifuge since the start of my Daemonic Money Magick course, and is perfect for any money magick, as he was put in charge of all the worldly treasures by order of Lucifer.

CHAPTER ELEVEN

The Fortune Sequence

This sequence was developed with the idea that many of us, if not most of us, often feel as if we were born "unlucky". Oh, we can have flashes of good luck, the occasional lottery or casino win, or even a small contest win, but mostly, that just doesn't happen to "us normal folks."

Then, there are those people who seem to go through life with luck alongside them the whole time. Mostly, my grandfather was a very lucky guy. He wasn't always lucky, but he always seemed to win those small contests like guessing the beans in a jar, having the winning raffle ticket, and those old-fashioned games at county fairs like the "cake walk". And he could have beaten anyone at checkers.

To get into the groove of being a winner, we have to purge the "loser" mindset, so that is the first step in the Fortune Sequence.

Then we look at blocks and remove them, first internal blocks (similar to mindset) and then external blocks.

Beginning with small steps, you will work multiple rituals to gain confidence not only in your own magick but also in the combined magick of The Seven. With each success comes more confidence.

This sequence, with the exceptions of the magick with the genius-spirits (covered at the end), is designed to be worked in order. Purging a mindset, removing both external and internal blocks, then preparing for the master ritual. This preparation isn't too involved, it's a ritual you work to simply get to know The Seven. I strongly advise against skipping forward to the master ritual. Even after decades of practice, I still have blockages which can prevent magick from occurring, so I am always working those block-removal rituals. So, we do these first.

After shifting your mindset, then removing blockages, we move on to some simple rituals designed to give you a taste for fortune magick that produces results. The idea of baby-steps might frustrate a few of you, but it's needed so that the master ritual is effective.

First up are three mindset exercises/rituals, two which use a regular ritual to a specific daemon who will help you with removing blocks, both internal and external, including those which may be only imaginary. Those types of blocks where you feel you are unlucky, but in reality it's only your mindset which is causing the bad luck.

CHAPTER TWELVE

Step One: Purging Your Mindset

This can be as simple as working several small rituals and gaining confidence in your magick, or as elaborate as doing some "mindset" purging exercises to help you convince yourself that you are "lucky" and a "winner".

Another method is to create a talisman that will act to purge these thoughts and reject any outside blocking energy aimed at you.

To make a talisman, either choose a Pentacle of Solomon, such as 1st Pentacle of the Moon, 5th Pentacle of Mercury, or 2nd Pentacle of Saturn.

Or, you can craft a sigil and have it turned into a talisman by fixing it in clay, or onto a wooden disc. Such a sigil is a simple matter to create.

Using a simple statement of desire, such as "I no longer have any blocks in my path," you can use the material in the Appendix to make a sigil.

Or an audio as mentioned in Chapter Seven.

Exercise to Banish the "Loser" Mindset

One simple exercise is to use an image which represents the "Loser" Mindset, and focus on that to purge that blocking "loser" energy.

This small ritual will need a candle or two, a red marker, and a fireproof bowl.

Using a simple drawing (below - it's also part of the downloads for this book on my site, see the Appendix)

Print this cartoon out.

Then, go to your altar, and set up a small, simple ritual. With only candles lit, look at the cartoon, then using a red marker, draw a RED slash through it.

On the back, write "I banish thee!" with the marker.

Stare at the cartoon, then touch the paper to a candle and shout at the image "I banish THEE!" while it burns.

Once it has been reduced to ashes, spit onto the ashes three times.

Once this is done, take the bowl outside and dump the ashes onto the ground, grinding the ashes into the earth with your foot. I mean, really GRIND the ashes. Banish those thoughts!

This exercise is done!

Blocks Removal Ritual to Marbas

Similar to a Road Opener, this ritual is designed to remove any energy that might prevent you from seeing success when playing games of chance, or while job hunting, or while searching for that perfect life partner, or if you feel there is "something" keeping you from being Fortunate.

For this, we will use Marbas. His daemonic powers are such, he can dramatically remove anyone who might prevent you from being fortunate. This might be someone around you who is always "down", walking around as if they have a cloud over their heads, always depressed and gloomy. It might be someone who is intentionally preventing you from seeing any good luck, or an actual curse.

In my personal experience, I had someone actively working against me, generating blocks. I asked Marbas to take care of this issue, and this person was removed from my life. Soon after the ritual, there was a rather dramatic email from this person, dropping all projects of mine that she was associated with.

Your petition can be worded as follows: *"President Marbas! I ask that you remove any and all blocking energy or any person who is actively acting against me or cursing me!"*

Offerings and sacrifices. For this simple ritual, I'd go with a small amount of wine or a spirit. Marbas also loves a raw egg, but a blood sacrifice is always good. If doing the blood sacrifice, have a diabetic lancet handy along with a spare copy of his sigil.

If using resin incense, also obtain some rosemary. Place a few dried leaves on the charcoal, as rosemary is an energy cleansing herb.

Items needed for this ritual:

- Altar candles
- Marbas Sigil
- Black candle (or green/black reversal candle)
- Incense such as Frankincense
- Offering and offering bowl
    o (If using a blood sacrifice, use a fireproof bowl)
- Uncrossing Oil
- Your petition
- Ritual directions

Set your altar up as you normally would, and in my case, I use a mix of white and black candles on either side of my altar, with the incense burner in the center, towards the back. Sigil is placed in front of the incense.

If using resin incense, light the charcoal and allow it to be fully going (ash coating), then light the altar candles. Do not light the black candle at this time.

Place a drop of the uncrossing oil on your hand, and coat the black candle with it. Set this aside.

Room lights go off.

Cast the circle. I summon the elements with specific daemons representing the elements.

Start by standing, looking north, then say:

Lirach Tasa Vefa Wehlic, Belial.

Turn and look east, and say:

Renich Tasa Uberaca Biasa Icar, Lucifer.

Turn and look south and say:

Ganic Tasa fubin, Flereous.

Turn to the west and say:

Jedan Tasa hoet naca, Leviathan.

Look up and invoke Satan:

Tasa reme laris Satan–Ave Satanis

Then define a circle with your finger, drawing a circle completely around you and your space.

You can walk around the altar, or if you have the altar against a wall, simple aim at the wall above the altar.

Then say:

Any energies existing in this space are now ejected, except those which I have called.

Now, it's time for the main part of this ritual.

Summon Marbas by saying his ENN three times:

Renach tasa uberace biasa icar Marbas! I summon thee, President Marbas!

Renach tasa uberace biasa icar Marbas! I summon thee, President Marbas!

Renach tasa uberace biasa icar Marbas! I summon thee, President Marbas!

Wait a few moments for his arrival.

If you are sensitive, you might feel his presence. Think about the blocks you are experiencing. Imagine how it will feel when the blocks dissolve. Feel the relief.

Now, pick up your petition and read it out loud.

Pick up the black candle, and hold it up over his sigil. **"President Marbas, I now ask that you enchant this candle to remove all blocking energies that are crossing my path!"**

Touch the black candle's wick to one of the other candles, and set it in a sturdy candle holder.

Sit back and meditate a few moments on the results of the ritual. Begin to feel a loosening of the surrounding energies. The tightness of the blocks is being removed, one by one.

Now, for the offering or sacrifice. If offering wine or another item, pick it up and hold it over Marbas' sigil. Then say something like

"I humbly offer you this _____ in gratitude for acting on my petition."

When offering wine or an egg, allow it to sit on Marbas' sigil for 24 hrs, then pour it out onto the ground, or place the object in nature.

If offering a blood sacrifice, using the diabetic lancet, prick a finger and place a single drop of blood onto his sigil. Then hold it up and say:

"President Marbas! In gratitude for your attending to my petition, I now give over to you this essence of my life."

Touch a corner of the paper to a candle flame, and allow the paper to burn completely in the fireproof bowl. Make sure it burns safely and use a spoon or other item to stir the ashes.

One more step. Time to dismiss Marbas and again, thank him for arriving and listening to your petition.

Say: **"President Marbas! I am honored by your presence, and I thank you for coming when I call. You may depart now in peace and please return when I call again! Guardians, I now dismiss you, as this ritual is now complete!"**

That's it.

Record in your journal when you performed this ritual, and track the results.

Road Opener

A road opener is often a set of rituals using a candle and a jar. Although I'll present some traditional elements, this road opener is simple and quite effective. If you can find it, you will need to acquire a special herb, known as Abre Camino, and use it to coat a candle, or infuse into an oil. You can also get this herb as a bath and cologne. What I do is I take the fresh herb and dry it, then it'll keep quite a while. My first batch I left in the bag and it went bad. So, the next bag I dried it.

If you use this with a candle, and it is a "7-day" votive, be extra cautious. Large bits can catch fire as they float in the wax, which can cause a house fire. I infuse it into an oil with essential oils (recipe in the appendix) and I use a metal skewer to poke a hole down the edge of the candle. Then I add a few drops of the oil to the hole, and allow it to drip down the candle. Now it's ready to use.

You can use any of The Seven in this ritual. My experience has been that Marbas is excellent at road openers, but Bael and Belphegor will also work wonders, so in this example, I'll be using Bael. If you wish to use another spirit, simply substitute ENNs and their name as needed below.

The petition. I have worded the petitions I have used like this: "King Bael! I ask now that you assist me in opening up all roads for my success in achieving (your task or goal). Remove people, remove energies, remove all obstacles!

Items needed:
- Standard altar candles
- Bael's sigil
- Road Opener oil or herbs
- Orange candle

- Incense (frankincense is good, if using a stick, go with traditional aromas like Nag Champa or Patchouli.)
- Fireproof Offering bowl
- Offering can be a blood sacrifice, but you can also use burnt meat or an egg.
- The petition

Prepare the candle by either dropping some road opener oil onto it, coating the candle, or dropping the oil into the votive candle.

Light the incense charcoal, then the candles once the incense is going.

Lights off

Settle yourself and cast the circle.

Start by standing, looking north, then say:

Lirach Tasa Vefa Wehlic, Belial.

Turn and look east, and say:

Renich Tasa Uberaca Biasa Icar, Lucifer.

Turn and look south and say:

Ganic Tasa fubin, Flereous.

Turn to the west and say:

Jedan Tasa hoet naca, Leviathan.

Look up and invoke Satan:

Tasa reme laris Satan–Ave Satanis

Then cast a circle with your finger, drawing the circle completely around you and your space.

You can walk around the altar, or if you have the altar against a wall, simply aim at the wall above the altar.

Then say:

Any energies existing in this space are now ejected, except those which I have called.

Now, it's time for the main part of this ritual.

Summon Bael by saying his ENN three times:

Ayer Secore On Ca Bael! I summon thee, King Bael!

Ayer Secore On Ca Bael! I summon thee, King Bael!

Ayer Secore On Ca Bael! I summon thee, King Bael!

Wait a few moments for his arrival.

If you are sensitive, you might feel his presence. Think about the blocks you are experiencing. Imagine how it will feel when the blocks dissolve. Feel the relief.

Now, pick up your petition and read it out loud.

Pick up the orange candle, and hold it up over his sigil. **"King Bael, I now ask that you enchant this candle to open up the road, clear the roads moving forward!"**

Touch the orange candle's wick to one of the other candles, and set it in a sturdy candle holder (*see my essay on "Candle Safety" in the appendix).

Sit back and meditate a few moments on the results of the ritual. Begin to feel a loosening of the surrounding energies. The tightness of the blocks are being removed, one by one.

Now, for the offering or sacrifice. If offering wine or another item, pick it up and hold it over Bael's sigil. Then say something like

"I humbly offer you all this _____ in gratitude for acting on my petition."

When offering wine or an egg, allow it to sit on Bael's sigil for 24 hrs, then pour it out onto the ground, or place the object in nature.

If offering a blood sacrifice, using the diabetic lancet, prick a finger and place a single drop of blood onto his sigil. Then hold it up and say:

"King Bael! In gratitude for your attending to my petition, I now give over to you this essence of my life."

Touch a corner of the paper to a candle flame, and allow the paper to burn completely in the fireproof bowl. Make sure it burns safely and use a spoon or other item to stir the ashes.

One more step. Time to dismiss Bael and again, thank him for arriving and listening to your petition.

Say: "King Bael! I am honored by your presence, and I thank you for coming when I call. You may depart now in peace and please return when I call again! Guardians, I now as that you depart, as this ritual is finished."

The ritual is now complete.

Record in your journal when you performed this ritual, and track the results.

CHAPTER THIRTEEN

Step Two: Baby Steps

A child will work its way up, from crawling to toddling, then to running. (Unless your child was like mine, and figured she had places to be, and pretty much skipped crawling.)

It's the same way with fortune magick. Start small. Win the minor games, small amounts, and work your way up.

Earlier, I mentioned how Native American casinos might be guarded by magick, and by working your way up, the magick you'll be working will overcome the magick designed to make you lose. One way past this is by working the block removal ritual and specifically ask Marbas to counter any magick aimed at your magick.

At all times, understand that this magick will assist you in winning, but it does not guarantee a win in every game.

Winner, Winner. Chicken Dinner.

You might have heard this saying. It's mostly associated with the southern, rural parts of the United States, often said at local carnivals or county fairs after playing one of the many games available at such a gathering. It's been said this phrase comes from back-alley gamblers during the Great Depression of the 1930s. These desperate gamblers would bet with whatever money they had, hoping to win a chicken dinner.

This is said after winning, but more likely said just before placing a bet or playing a game.

With this short introductory ritual, this phrase can be enchanted to actually work. (I just tested this, and won small on an online scratch-off game).

Using the special "Fortune" sigil, we'll summon Belphegor, using the standard summoning, plus an older, archaic way of energizing the sigil and then the phrase, "Winner, Winner, Chicken, Dinner" is enchanted for use.

The petition is pretty easy: "Prince Belphegor! Hear my prayer! I ask that you now assist me in winning (name the game)."

Preparation - using a small gold candle, coat it with the oil, place it in a sturdy holder, and then sprinkle it with cinnamon or powdered bay leaves.

Work this ritual before you go out to gamble or play the lottery. It's one of the few rituals you can work many times.

Items needed:

- Altar candles

- Fortune Master Sigil
- Gold candle that you have prepared
- Symbol from the game you want to play (casino chip, lottery slip, etc.)
- Piece of paper with "Winner, winner, chicken dinner" written on it
- Fortune incense (or something like Nag Champa)
- Fortune Oil or Gambler's Luck Oil
- Offering to Belphegor can be a piece of sweet cake or bread, honey, pile of sugar.

Summoning:

Lyan Ramec Catya Ganen Belphegor! I summon thee, Prince Belphegor!

Lyan Ramec Catya Ganen Belphegor! I summon thee, Prince Belphegor!

Lyan Ramec Catya Ganen Belphegor! I summon thee, Prince Belphegor!

Be with me and grace me with your energy!

I now ask that - (read your petition)

After reading your petition, hold up the sigil or talisman and say: **Belphegor! Hoc symbolum fascinare me fortunae adferre!**

Pause for a few breaths. Then, look at the symbol from the game (lotto slip, etc.) and meditate on winning! *See the money flowing to you!*

Look at the words *"Winner! Winner! Chicken Dinner!"* and

see the money flowing to you. Tell yourself that each time you see these words, you are a winner!

Hold your hand over the altar, the sigil and words, the play-slips and candle, and say,

Into this sigil and into these play slips (chips, cards) I now project great power! Power drawn from you, Prince Belphegor, and power from within myself. These symbols now possess great power! Power to alter my life forever! Power to WIN!

Pause and catch your breath. Now, the offering.

Oh Belphegor! I thank you for your grace and attention to my prayers. I further pray that you see I win! And I win BIG. In gratitude, I hereby offer to you (*your offering*)**.**

Place the offering in the center of the altar.

Oh Belphegor! I now give you leave to depart. Depart in peace and come again when I next call!

Allow the offering to stay on your altar overnight, then place it into nature.

Keep the enchanted sigil with you when you next go to play the lottery or gamble.

(Note: *Hoc symbolum fascinare me fortunae adferre* is supposed to mean "Enchant this fortune sigil…")

CHAPTER FOURTEEN

Step Three: Preparing for the Master Ritual

Preparation is straight forward. Obtain the ritual items needed, add any you see fit to add, and buy and make the incense blends, and first contact the Seven, during which one daemon will come forward as the spokesman for the other daemons.

The Incense

The Seven are traditional Goetic beings, in that they prefer the usual trappings for a ritual. This means real incense. Obtain a small amount, one or two ounces, of the following resins: Frankincense tears, Dragon's Blood, white copal, and on occasion you may also want to add some sweet myrrh.

Dragon's Blood comes in rather large hunks, so what I do is crush a bit with some pliers, and use the small bits in the blend.

Don't powder the incense, just crush it a bit.

The base blend is as follows:

- *Three parts Frankincense*
- *One part Dragon's Blood*
- *One part white copal*

I combine the incense, and store it in either a small resealable plastic bag or in a small jar. Shake well, and use a small teaspoon in the ritual to place a small amount on the burning charcoal.

Master Gold Candle

Go locate and purchase a large gold candle. Not the same candle used with The Lady, but similar. I have a 4-inch (10cm) round pillar, about 6 inches (35cm) high. If you have artistic talent, you can also draw the Master Sigil on the candle.

Offering or Sacrifice

The offering can be anything that represents life, such as a bit of raw meat, a bit of cooked meat (AKA burnt offerings, or in Texas, smoked barbecue) or a raw egg.

A sacrifice is usually a small drop of blood.

So, which should you use in the Master Ritual?

Bune, his-own-self, has suggested the following:

Everyday things, such as a bit of cash, or a chance at a new job, an offering works. For major stuff, like life-changing amounts of money, a sacrifice is suggested.

So, yes, while working the Master Ritual, you are to do a blood offering. It's painless (sorta) and quick. I have an alcohol prep pad with me, as well as a diabetic lancet. I use the ring finger on my left hand, just below the tip. I have found I have a small area where the nerves aren't as sensitive. I poke myself there, and a small drop of blood results.

ONLY one small drop of blood. No need to open a vein and bleed all over the sigils. If you find you are bleeding a lot (like if you are on blood thinners) then capture the excess with a small vial and use it to make "Magick Ink", which is useful for writing the petition.

The Petition

As in my other books, I advise that your petition be short and simple. Something like: "I win a lottery jackpot" is sufficient unless you want to play for a major multi-state major win, in that case say that: "I win a jackpot in the (X) lottery!"

I'd leave out the exact name of the lottery because you might win one you don't normally play.

If you are planning a trip to a casino, then word the petition like this: "I win BIG while playing…" then fill in the details, such as Blackjack, slots, craps, or the midget car races.

The Pre-Ritual Master Ritual

This is a ritual you should work prior to working the main ritual. Sounds silly, but you need to do some work with The Seven before gathering them all together and asking for huge magick, such as a lottery win or that perfect job complete with a corner office and a view. This ritual will also introduce you to the one spirit who steps forward as the spokesperson of the group. This is who you can summon in subsequent rituals when you begin to refine the magick or need feedback on progress.

This is also where you will need to use some method to get answers and feedback on your desires and potential paths to manifest that desire. I prefer to use the pendulum, and I have instructions on making a pendulum, as well as answer charts, in the Appendix.

This ritual has the blood sacrifice as *optional*. So, if you decide to pass up on the sacrifice, I suggest a small amount of good whiskey or other liquor, or a fresh, raw egg (in the shell). Raw beef is also acceptable. Leave the offering in the offering vessel overnight, then place it into nature.

Items needed:

- Master Sigil
- Small Master Sigil for offering
- Altar Candles
- Master Gold Candle
- Incense blend
- Room to work and a printout of this ritual
- Pendulum or other communicating device
- Paper and pen for recording the answers
- Offering/Sacrifice (Diabetic lancet for blood offering)

- Fireproof bowl or offering bowl

When ready, light the candles, start the charcoal, and turn off the room lights.

Once the charcoal is burning, glowing and covered in white ash, place a small amount of the incense on the burner, and allow the smoke to rise, cleansing the energy in the room.

Once this is done, cast a circle.

Start by standing, looking north, then say:

Lirach Tasa Vefa Wehlic, Belial.

Turn and look east, and say:

Rancher Tasa Uberaca Biasa Icar, Lucifer.

Turn and look south and say:

Ganic Tasa fubin, Flereous.

Turn to the west and say:

Jedan Tasa hoet naca, Leviathan.

Look up and invoke Satan:

Tasa reme laris Satan–Ave Satanis

Then define a circle with your finger, drawing a circle completely around you and your space. If you have room, you can walk around the altar, or if you have the altar against a wall, simply aim at the wall above the altar.

Then say:

Any energies existing in this space are now ejected, except those which I have called.

Now, it's time for the main part of this ritual.

Sit or stand, and face north.

Summon the Seven by saying:

Ayer Secore On Ca Bael! I summon thee, King Bael!

Rean ganen ayar da Agares! I summon thee, Duke Agares!

Renach tasa uberace biasa icar Marbas! I summon thee, President Marbas!

Wehl melan avage Bune Tasa! I summon thee, Duke Bune!

Lyan Ramec Catya Ganen Belphegore! I summon thee, Prince Belphegore!

Tasa Mammon on ca lirach! I summon thee, Mammon!

Eyen Tasa Valocur Lucifuge Rofocal! I summon thee, Lucifuge!

Wait a few moments for The Seven to assemble. The room might feel a bit crowded, especially to those who are a bit psychic. Once you feel they all are present, address them like this:

Friends, I have asked you all to be with me in my space, at this time, so that I may prepare for the Master Ritual. I will now ask a few questions, and await your answers, using this pendulum to get your answers.

(At this point, begin asking questions to get a feel for what can be accomplished towards your goal, and how to apply this magick. It's open ended, potentials everywhere, and the Master Ritual can be revised to fit almost any need. More later!)

At this time, you can ask to see which of the Seven will come forward as the Spokesman for the group:

Friends, thank you for your answers. I have one last request, and that is I wish for one of you to come forward to act as spokesman for the rest of the group. Will one of you come forward?

Use the pendulum with the prepared chart with their names, so see who is coming forward. If you get no clear answer, you may ask this question again in another ritual.

It is time to give the offering or blood sacrifice. Use the words below which best fit the offering.

Friends, I thank you for being with me in my space at this time and for your answers. In return, I hereby offer a drop of my essence.

Prick your finger, and allow a single drop of blood to drop onto the small sigil. Then pick this up and touch it to a candle flame, and allow it to burn completely in the fireproof bowl.

If offering something else, say something like this:

Friends, I thank you for being with me in my space and for answering my questions. In return, I ask that you please accept his humble offering of _____.

Place the offering into the bowl, and place it on their large sigil.

Now, close the ritual with this:

Friends, our ritual is now over. I ask that you depart in peace, having arrived in peace. Please come again when I next call. Since this ritual is now done, I ask that the guardians I have called now depart, and I thank them for their help.

The ritual is now completed.

Next, using your answers, get prepared to work the Master Ritual.

CHAPTER FIFTEEN

The Master Ritual

This is where it all comes together. Until now, you have worked with only one or two spirits at a time, manifesting small things and removing anything (or anyone) standing in your way. Now, we get down to some serious magick.

Unlike the earlier rituals, everything I list below is absolutely necessary to this Master Ritual. Even down to the offerings suggested. So, settle yourself on the fact you will need to burn a specific resin on an incense charcoal burner, and that you will need actual gold candles. Only option I can give is in what form the Master Sigil is used. A simple print-out on paper is sufficient. If you can get a talisman created (see Appendix) then you can easily carry this sigil around with you while you do the physical work of making the desire manifest.

You must also work this ritual prior to working the

pathworking.

Otherwise, you may find only one or two of the summoned daemons to have actually arrived, and the magick has a much harder time to work. It might give you small manifestations, or partially manifest, but your ultimate goal will remain out of your reach.

During the preparation for this ritual, you will have defined your goal, or desire, and you should have made copies of the Master Sigil. If you had a talisman made, use this in the ritual.

This ritual can, and should be, modified to accomplish any fortune or gambling magick you may wish to work, and I figure you can modify this master ritual for most anything, up to and including love and defeating an enemy. This ritual can also be worked many times, before going gambling or buying lottery tickets, applying for a job, etc.

Items needed:
- Master Sigil
- Small Master Sigil for offering
- Altar Candles
- Master Gold Candle
- Incense blend
- Item to represent your goal (lotto slip, cards, resume, etc)
- Room to work and a printout of this ritual
- Offering/Sacrifice (Diabetic lancet for blood offering)

- Offering bowl
- Fireproof bowl

When ready, light the candles, start the charcoal, and turn off the room lights.

Once the charcoal is burning, glowing and covered in white ash, place a small amount of the incense on the charcoal, and allow the smoke to rise, cleansing the energy in the room.

Once this is done, cast a circle.

Start by standing, looking north, then say:

Lirach Tasa Vefa Wehlic, Belial.

Turn and look east, and say:

Rancher Tasa Uberaca Biasa Icar, Lucifer.

Turn and look south and say:

Ganic Tasa fubin, Flereous.

Turn to the west and say:

Jedan Tasa hoet naca, Leviathan.

Look up and invoke Satan:

Tasa reme laris Satan–Ave Satanis

Then use your finger to draw a circle completely around you and your space. If you have room, you can walk around the altar, or if you have the altar against a wall, simple aim at the wall above the altar.

Then say:

Any energies existing in this space are now ejected, except those which I have called.

Now, it's time for the main part of this ritual.

Sit or stand, and face north.

Summon the Seven by saying:

Ayer Secore On Ca Bael! I summon thee, King Bael!

Rean ganen ayar da Agares! I summon thee, Duke Agares!

Renach tasa uberace biasa icar Marbas! I summon thee, President Marbas!

Wehl melan avage Bune Tasa! I summon thee, Duke Bune!

Lyan Ramec Catya Ganen Belphegore! I summon thee, Prince Belphegore!

Tasa Mammon on ca lirach! I summon thee, Mammon!

Eyen Tasa Valocur Lucifuge Rofocal! I summon thee Lucifuge!

Pause a moment, and allow their energy to surround you. Begin to visualize what it is you wish to manifest. Go into details here. Money in the bank. What you can buy with large amounts of money? Lottery win. Gambling and winning BIG. That perfect job. The perfect life partner.

At this point, take up your petition you have written and read it aloud.

Now, light the Master Gold candle and wait a moment. Then, touch the petition to the candle's flame and say,

With the burning of this petition, a pact is sealed.

Allow the petition to burn fully in the fire-proof bowl. (I use a long tea spoon to lift the paper, to allow it to completely burn)

Take a moment to meditate on the outcome. Fully visualize your desire manifesting. Go into detail and take your time.

Pause and take a deep breath.

Time for the offering. In this Master Ritual, it is highly advised to use a blood offering.

Place the small Master Sigil in the center of the altar, and take the diabetic lancet, and prick a finger. Allow ONE drop of blood to drop into the sigil. (If you have extra bleeding, capture this in a small vial for use in making magick ink or for signing a pact later)

Allow the drop to dry, then hold up the sigil and address it:

Please accept my essence, in return for your favor!

At this point touch the sigil to a candle flame, dropping the burning paper into a fire-proof bowl. Stir the ashes to make sure the sigil has burned completely. The next day, drop the ashes onto the ground.

To close the ritual, sit back and look at the master sigil, and stack the lotto play slips on the sigil, then hold your hand over them and visualize golden light flowing form your hands into the items.

Next say:

Into this Sigil/talisman and into this (chip, playslips, etc) I now project great power. Power drawn from the great spirits around me, and power drawn from inside me. I charge these talismans to bring me grand luck, jackpot wins, and fabulous fortune! So it is written, so it is done!

Hold this image for a few moments, and relax. Sit back and dismiss The Seven.

I am done. This ritual is done. The magick is powerful, and I give thanks to you all for attending to my petition. You may depart, and come again when I next call. Since this ritual is now done, I ask that the guardians I have called now depart, and I thank them for their help.

Sit in meditation for a few more moments. The ritual is finished.

Extinguish the candles, including the master gold candle. If you are using a spell candle with this ritual, allow it to burn out completely.

Pathworking The Seven

Work this only after doing all the preparation and the Master Ritual. This type of pathworking, like the ones to The Lady, can be worked in a hotel room, vacant bathroom, or in your car. All is needed is the sigil and some quiet time.

You will need your petition, and expect to leave a sacrifice on the Seven's Master sigil. The daemon who is the spokes-daemon for the group will be the one who will appear first in this pathworking. The others may hang back, or may not even let their presence be known, but they will be listening and lending their power to your magick.

For this pathworking, you should have worked the physical master ritual first. Although no results are guaranteed, I can assure you that not working the main ritual first will cause this one to fail. Trust me.

Initially, you will just need the master sigil or talisman made from the master sigil. If you are in a space where you can use a candle, then do so.

Settle yourself in and go into an alpha state.

When ready, visualize the following:

A dark sky, devoid of stars.

Off in the distance, a glow of gold.

Closer now, see a pathway lit by bright gold coins along the edge.

Walk down this path.

The path now opens out to a large, paved circle, all lit by glowing coins.

In your mind, call out "I am here"

The spokesman for The Seven will appear. You can present your petition or ask questions at this time.

You can also ask that the sigil or talisman be energized again, if you feel its power has diminished after the first time it was energized.

After presenting your petition and receiving answers, it's time to close this ritual. In your mind, give thanks to the Seven and tell them you're departing now.

Visualize the following to end the ritual:

You turn, and walk back along the path.

As you leave, the gold coins shift, lighting your way home.

Once you exit the pathway, the ritual is done.

As soon as you can after completing the path, leave the Seven an offering of a single drop of your blood on a small copy of the Master Sigil.

Touch the sigil to a candle flame and allow it to burn completely.

CHAPTER SIXTEEN

Money Spirits/Genius Spirits

In magick, there are quite a few spirits who are not classified as "daemons" and who can assist practitioners with manifesting desires. After the Master Ritual, I figured to go over a couple, one you might have heard of already, Nitika, and another who is a bit more obscure, Ataphiel, a spirit who only makes a single appearance in an old magick book by Frater Malak, AKA Geof Gray-Cobb. It's an interesting, if out-of-date book, and the rituals are a bit complicated and involved. I have simplified the summoning of Ataphiel and it now fits in with basic high magick, along with a sigil which enables the magician to make quick contact without all the fuss of other methods.

Nitika

Nitika is a genius spirit, a spirit of wealth and gemstones. Like Ataphiel, he/she is first encountered in an older magick book by Geof Gray-Cobb. In my other book on Daemons, I go over the use of Nitika, along with a new, awesome sigil. It is felt by my readers that the new sigil is quite powerful, so it is used here.

Nitika is a general use wealth spirit, and can be worked as a full mental ritual, or as a physical magick ritual. In the physical ritual, Nitika's candles are usually yellow, but I personally use my white pillar candles, so white can be used if you do not have, or feel like buying, more candles. Everything else is the same as in a standard ritual.

Nitika is quite easy to work with, and any incense you have on hand works. I personally light a few sticks of Nag Champa to fill my space with that spicy aroma, which reminds me of the new age shops in Austin back in the late 1970s.

A perfect petition is one where you simply ask Nitika to increase your fortune by making you lucky in all areas of your life.

The base ritual to Nitika is the one I used in my other books and uses the binding phrases which work best for Nitika, where you say the sacred words of the Abrahamic deity, YHWH. The name YHWH, consisting of the sequence of consonants Yod, Heh, Waw, and Heh, is known as the tetragrammaton.

- Nitika's sigil.

Items needed:Candle. One or more. Yellow, if not, then white.

- Offering: Anything of nature. Herbs, flowers, and fruit. I have also offered liquor and wine.

- Incense. Use a money draw incense, or any incense you prefer

Set out your items on a small table. If you wish an altar cloth, ANY altar cloth will do. I once used a green bath towel.

Candle center. Sigil near candle.

Incense to one side and additional candles as desired.

Start the incense and allow the smoke to spread out.

Light candles and turn off room lights

Cast a circle. This is optional, but it is suggested to prevent the arrival of any unwanted spirits.

Breathe and gaze at the sigil. With a finger, trace the center part of the sigil while whispering or chanting over and over:

YOD-HAY-VOW-HAY

After tracing the sigil, place it so that it is easy to look at.

Chant three times:

EE-AH-OH-YEH

Now, call Nitika. Say his name three times!

KNEE-TEA-KAH

Now, the main call:

I summon you, Nitika, by the power of ELL, ELL-OH-HEEM, ADD-OH-NIGH ADD-EAR-EAR-ORN and EL-SHAD-EYE.

By the power of DYE NAH-MISS

I ask that you join with me.

I ask that hear me and grant me my desire.

Now say the following:

I ask that you alter the past and the future to bring me wealth. You are the Genius of Wealth, and I ask that you bestow upon me gold and great wealth.

Nitika, I ask that (read petition)

Pause a few moments here. Visualize your desire manifesting. Gambling wins, chips stacking up, slot machines dumping coins into your lap, etc.

In gratitude for your help, Nitika, I now humbly offer you (state your offering)

Now, ask for Nitika to depart:

Nitika, I ask now that you depart, as you came in peace, I ask that you depart in peace, and come again when I next call you.

Place the offering on the sigil, unless it's incense. In that case—hold sigil over incense and allow the smoke to waft around the sigil.

That's it. You're done.

The next day, take any offering (except the incense) outside and leave it for nature.

Ataphiel

I label this one as a genius spirit, and I have picked up this spirit is somewhat feminine, so I'll be referring to Ataphiel as "her". Her name is pronounced AH-TAH-FEE-ALE. With the emphasis on the TAH.

I first encountered her in an older text of rituals, with a very archaic and complex ritual with some lengthy preparations prior to performing the ritual. So, I went into her usual ritual and talked with her, and the following ritual is the result. She suggested I use the two "power" words to summon her, and those are incorporated into the ritual, and that we treat her as we would any other daemonic spirit.

Ataphiel's powers are aimed primarily at gambling, contests and card games. A good counterpart would be the goddess Fortune/Tyche. And like Fortuna, colors matter.

Candle colors need to be shades of green. If using a fountain pen to write your petition, do so using shades of green, with a drop of your own blood to make it a magick ink.

Use a drop of the Money Draw oil and coat the green spell candle with it during the ritual.

The basic High Magick ritual is perfect for making contact and asking for help in winning a specific game or lottery.

Ataphiel's altar candles can be green or a white. Print her sigil onto green paper, or use green ink to color the sigil.

The best incense is Morning Star Patchouli, followed by a white sage/palo santo mix. The Money Luck incense can also be used.

Offerings can be wine, bread, or flowers, but I was advised that if you are asking for a large favor, then use a blood offering.

Items needed are:

- Altar Candles
- TWO copies of Ataphiel's sigil, one small, one large
- Green spell candle
- Money or Fortune oil
- Offering
- Offering bowl
- Incense
- Lottery play slips or playing cards
- Diabetic lancet and fireproof bowl for blood offering.

Light the incense, then the candles. Cast a basic circle using the standard daemonic circle casting and banish any outside energies.

When ready, get quiet and put a drop of the oil onto your fingers and spread it on the small green spell candle. Place it into a solid holder and summon Ataphiel.

Genius Spirit Summoning as Daemon:

Ah-Bah-Lim! Mee-Sah-Boo! Ataphiel! I summon thee
By the powers of Jupiter and Venus!
By the power of El and Elohim,
By the powers of Ah-Bah-Lim and Mee-Sah-Boo!
I call to thee, Ataphiel!
Answer my call, and hear my prayers!

Pause a moment, as Ataphiel's energy should be with you. Try to sense the subtle vibrations in the air around your space.

Breathe slowly and go into the alpha state. Pick up the lottery play slip or deck of cards. *Fully visualize winning!* Focus on this, and say:

Ataphiel! I ask now that you guide me! I intend to manifest a major prize (or card game win). I ask now that you assist me making it happen NOW!

Sit back and again, visualize winning. *See the money flow to you!* Put the play slip or cards down and pick up the small sigil.

Now say:

Ataphiel! I now ask that you enchant this symbol that bears your divine design, empowering this symbol to bring to me major wins in all games that I play!

Pause for a few moments, and allow GREEN energy to appear in your hands and enter into the sigil. Watch the energy swirl around the sigil's lines and symbols.

After a period of at least 20 breaths, put the sigil back on the altar and pick up the offering, and say:

Ataphiel! In thanks for being with me in my space and for energizing me with the power of luck and winning, I humbly offer to you this _____.

Place the offering into a small bowl and place it on the larger sigil.

If offering blood, pick up the diabetic lancet and prick a finger. Place a single drop of blood onto her small sigil, and hold it up, saying:

Ataphiel! To you I now humbly offering my own essence, my sacred blood, in return for your favor!

Touch the sigil with the blood to a candle and allow it to burn completely in the fireproof bowl.

Finish the ritual by saying:

Ataphiel! I thank you for joining with me, and I ask now that you depart in peace, and please return when I next call on you!

Allow the offering to stay on her sigil overnight, then place the offering outside.

Keep the small, enchanted sigil with you while playing any lottery or gambling games.

The Master Sigils

The Lady Master Sigil

The Lady

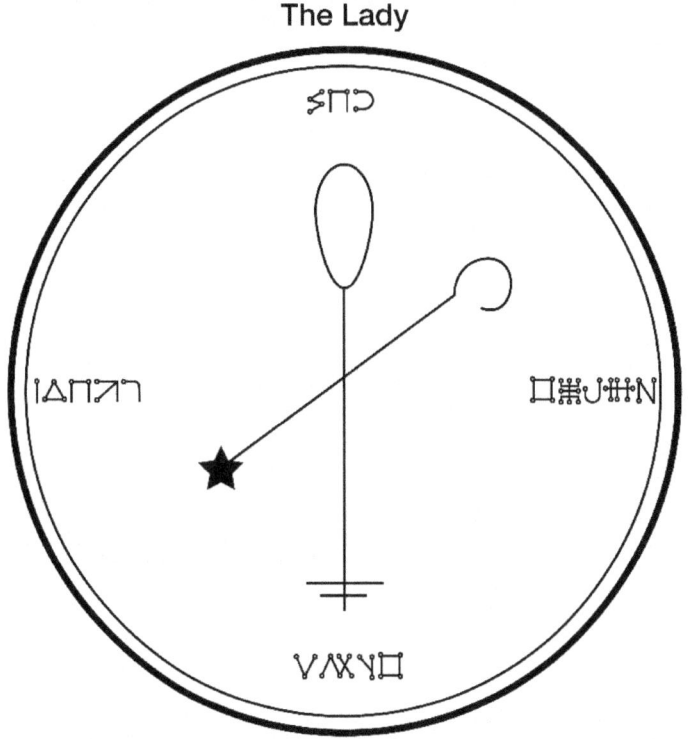

The Lady Candle Sigil

This is a simplified version of The Lady's main sigil. Trace this onto the side of a 3" (7.5 cm) golden candle with a permanent marker or enamel paint.

The Seven Master Candle

Master Sigil

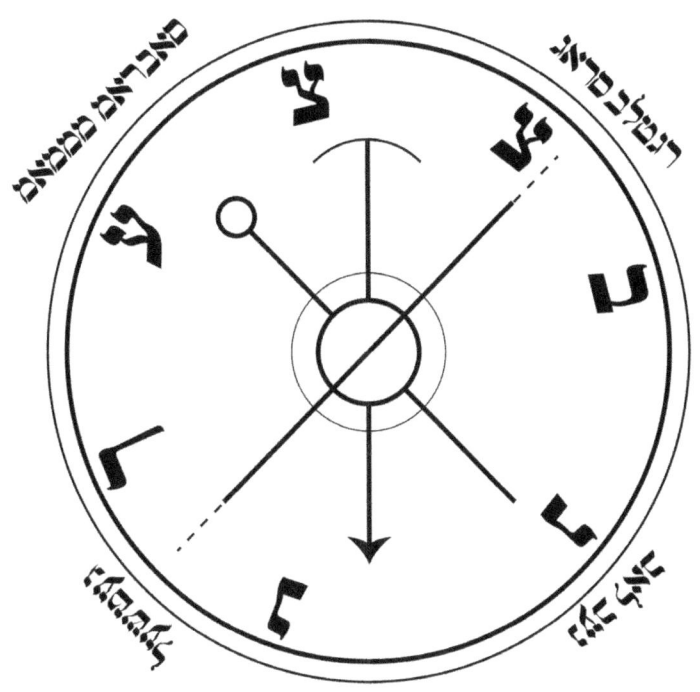

The Seven Master Sigil for the candle

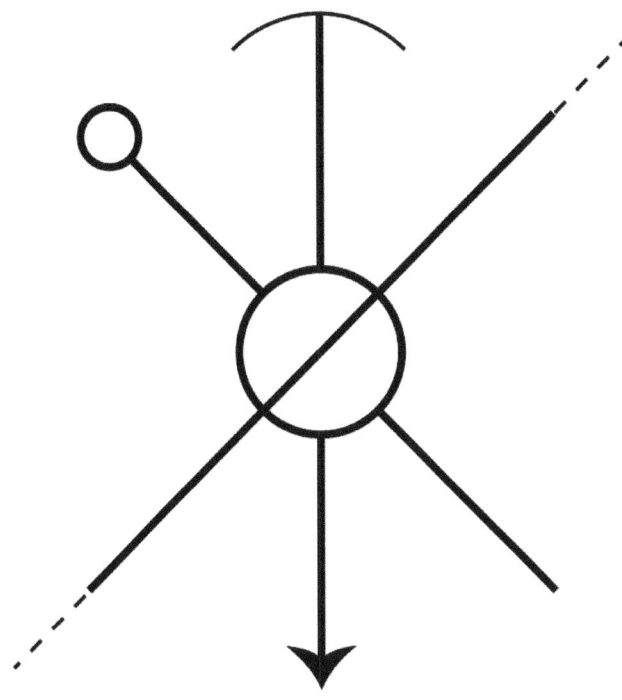

DAVID THOMPSON

Nitika

Nitika

DAVID THOMPSON

Ataphiel

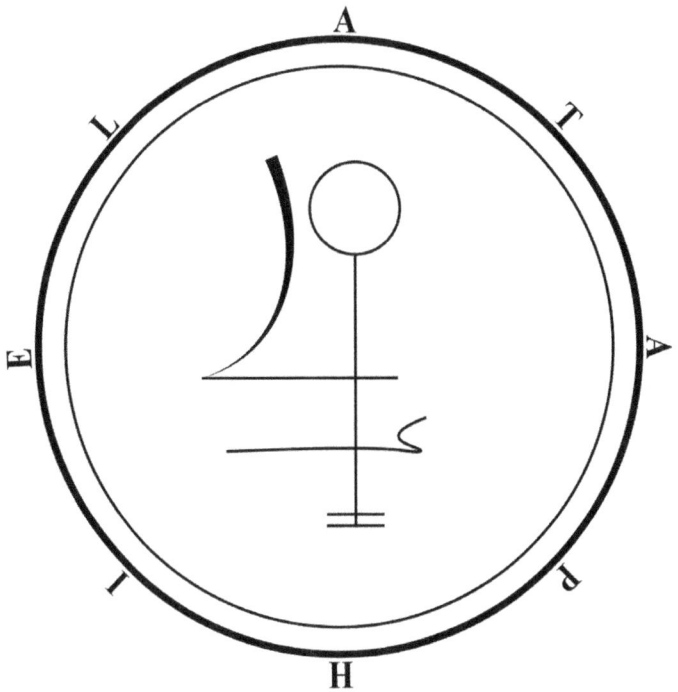

Fortune Master Sigil

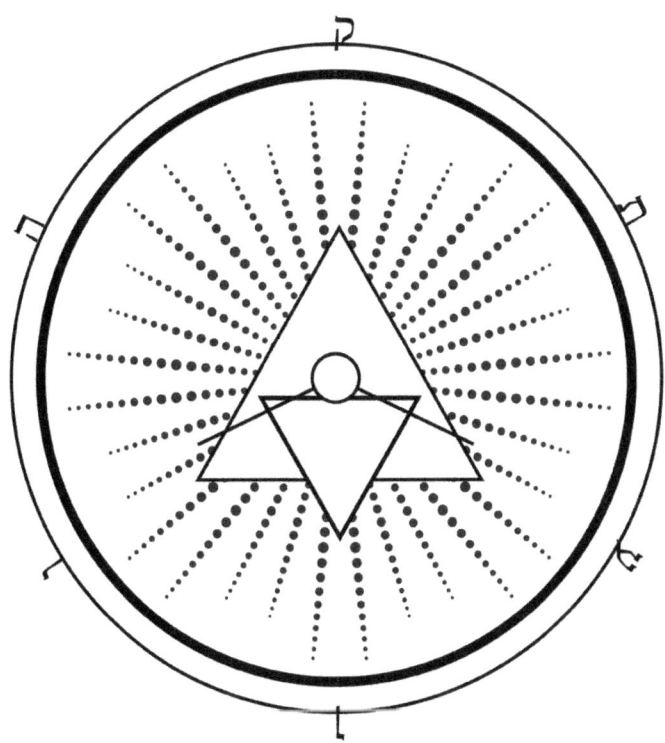

Luck Master Sigil

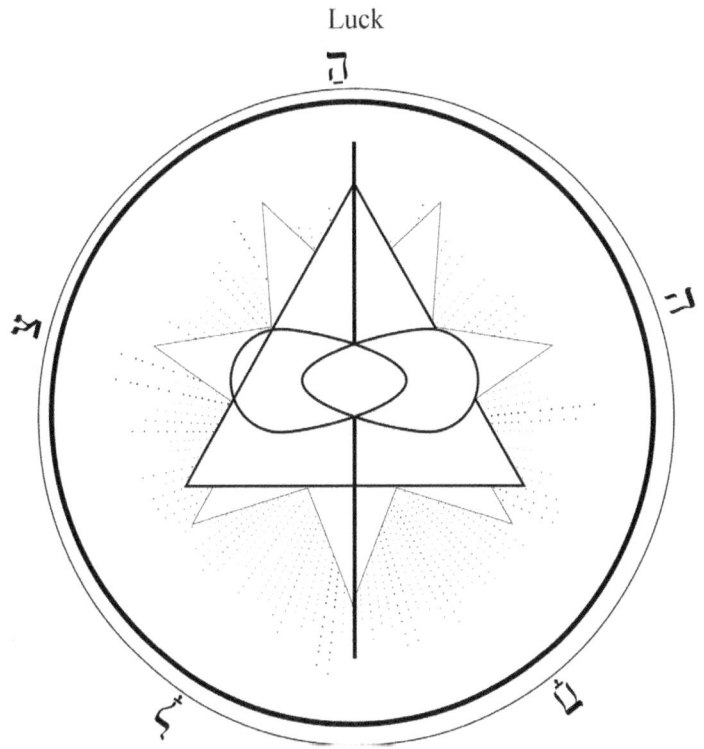

Power Sigil

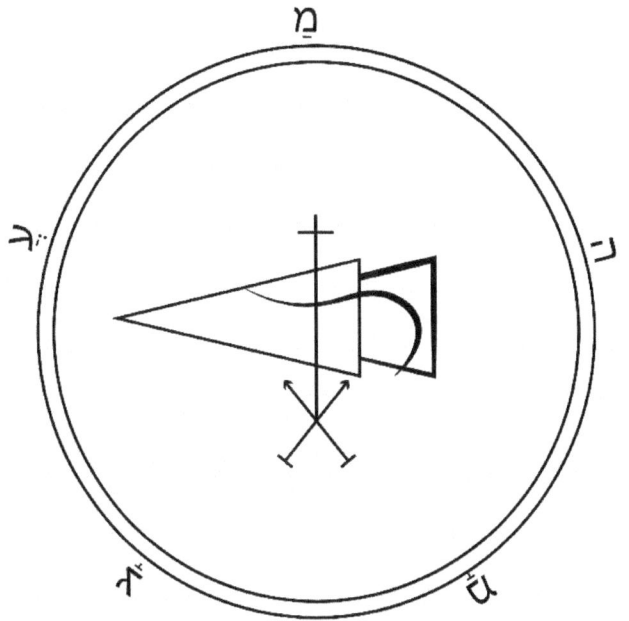

David Thompson

APPENDIX

Guided Meditations

I got my start meditating using cassette tapes I'd bought at a new age shop in south Austin.

These were by author Dick Sutphen, who had written a lot of material about mind programming, and held seminars on subjects like psychic powers, hypnosis, and past life therapy.

Eventually, these tapes were released on CD, then MP3 audios. In 2000 and 2001, I took two of his seminars and met with him, exploring this concept further.

He passed in 2020, and his audio library is now being handled by Hay House, and from there you can locate "The Awesome Power of Luck" and all his other audios. I highly recommend them. You can also check Amazon and Spotify.

I've posted a few guided meditations that I've found to be highly effective in inducing an altered state on my website. I recorded these using what I discovered from him and his seminars.

Links to audios are:

My line of altered state audios:

https://davepsychic.com/self-hypnosis-audios/

Dick Sutphen Audios can be found at

https://www.hayhouse.com/authorbio/dick-sutphen

Other Useful Links

Link for all the Sigils needed in this book, all in one PDF for easy downloading and printing:

https://davepsychic.com/fortunemastersigils/

I have placed links for most supplies needed in this book on my website

https://davepsychic.com/magick-supplies-links/

The list is sorted by item category.

Herbs and Oils

There are many online outlets for herbs and oils.

High John the Conqueror root:

https://www.originalbotanica.com/high-john-the-conqueror-root/

Oil of success: https://www.originalbotanica.com/liga-de-exito/

Abre Camino https://www.originalbotanica.com/fresh-abre-camino-plant/

Recipes for Incense and Oils.

Incense:

Lady Luck incense:
- 1 part crushed frankincense
- 1 part crushed myrrh
- 1 part cinnamon powder
- 1 part powdered bay leaves
- 1 part patchouli powder

Mix well, and place on hot coal. Be cautious with the smoke, as cinnamon can irritate the eyes. Store in an air-tight container.

Fortune Incense:
- 1 part crushed frankincense
- 1 part powdered cloves
- 1 part dried and crushed pine tree needles
- 1 part powdered nutmeg
- 1 part powdered ginger root

Mix all well, and place on hot coal. Will keep well in an air-tight container.

For oils, use any light oil as a base. Almond oil works, and so does mineral oil.

Money and Fortune Oils

Money Bring Oil:

To 1/4 cup (60ml) base oil add

- 4 drops of cinnamon oil
- 4 drops patchouli oil
- 4 drops sandalwood oil (substitute powder if no oil handy)
- Several crushed cloves
- Several pine needles chopped very fine

Mix well, and store in an air-tight bottle for three weeks in darkness. It's ready to use after 3 weeks. Do not filter or strain the oil.

Fortune Oil (essential oil version):

To 1/4 cup (60 ml) of base oil, add:

- 4 drops cinnamon oil
- 4 drops vanilla oil
- 4 drops wintergreen oil
- 4 drops spearmint oil

Allow the oils to mix completely and keep in a small bottle with a tight lid or screw top.

(*Note, it's hard to find vanilla oil. Do NOT use Vanilla extract. Try to find Vanilla Absolute, or infuse some vanilla beans to create your own oil.)

Fortune oil (herbs version):

To 1/4 cup (60ml) of base oil, add:

Crushed cinnamon

Crushed vanilla beans

Wintergreen leaves

Spearmint leaves

Crush the leaves with the cinnamon and vanilla beans, pack into a small jar, and cover with the base oil. Allow this to sit in a window with a lot of light for a few weeks.

Gambler's Luck Oil:

To 1/4 cup (60ml) of base oil, add:

3 drop cinnamon oil

1 part carnation petals

1 part anise seed or 3 drops oil

Add a piece of High John the Conqueror Root (see links)

Road Opener Oil

To 1/4 (60ml) cup base oil, add:

Crushed abre camino.

Add 4 drops of orange essential oil

Add 4 drops of Cedar Oil

Crushed sage

Mint

Allow this to steep in the oil for three weeks, then use. Shake it well, then put a few drops where it's needed.

Uncrossing Oil

To 1/4 cup (60ml) base oil, add:

4 drops Lemon Oil

4 drops Rose Oil

4 drops Lily Oil

1 drop Bay Oil or 2 crushed Leaves

Mix and allow to steep for two weeks, then bottle. Shake before use.

Crown of Success Oil

To 1/4 cup (60ml) base oil, add:

Allspice powder

Bergamot Orange oil

Bay oil

Clove oil

Cinnamon oil

Mix one part of each into the base oil, allow to steep for a few weeks, then put in a small bottle.

Other Oils

Come to me oil:

1/4 cup base oil

- 2 drops rose geranium
- 2 drops Oil of sweetpea.
- Herbs to add:

- rose petals
- Queen Elizbeth root
- patchouli leaf

Mix, cap in a small bottle and let set a few weeks.

Circle Casting

A circle is less for protection, and more for defining a special space where you can communicate with the spirits you are summoning.

The way I cast a circle all depends on what type of ritual I am doing. The daemonic ritual is the one I do the most often, where I will face east, summon Lucifer, then go to each direction, summoning a daemon who will act as a representative of that direction.

In other forms of magick, I define my circle by either walking around the altar, or by standing in the center, and aim my finger out, drawing a line in the air. I allow this line to drop to the floor, creating a line of golden energy, which will then form the circle.

I then eject all uninvited energies out of the space by sweeping my arms in a circle, as if sweeping those energies away, then I hold out my arms and say, "All uninvited energies and spirits and beings are now ejected, and will not be allowed within my space unless invited.

You can also preform the Lesser Banishing of the Pentagram, if you so wish.

Complex Sigils Creation

Some people will try to convince you that sigil creation is some type of complicated process and is all occult and ultra-top secret.

The information is all out there (meaning the interwebs) so what I am about to show you here isn't new, isn't some wild idea of my own, it's been used for well over 125 years. (Like the term "magick" or "magik", sheesh!)

Once you have a summary of your desire, phrased as a "past tense" statement, you will have a sentence of about 5 to 10 words.

Past tense simply means you phrase a desire as if it has already occurred.

A statement such as "I have one million dollars" would be a good example.

A statement such as "I wish to receive a huge sum of money" isn't a good example.

It's in future tense, uses a soft way of asking, "wish" and the money request isn't well defined.

Forget about HOW the money will come to you, you already have it.

So, taking this statement, you'd look at what letters exist, then cross out each vowel (and I include the vowel "y" in this).

Thus, the following happens:

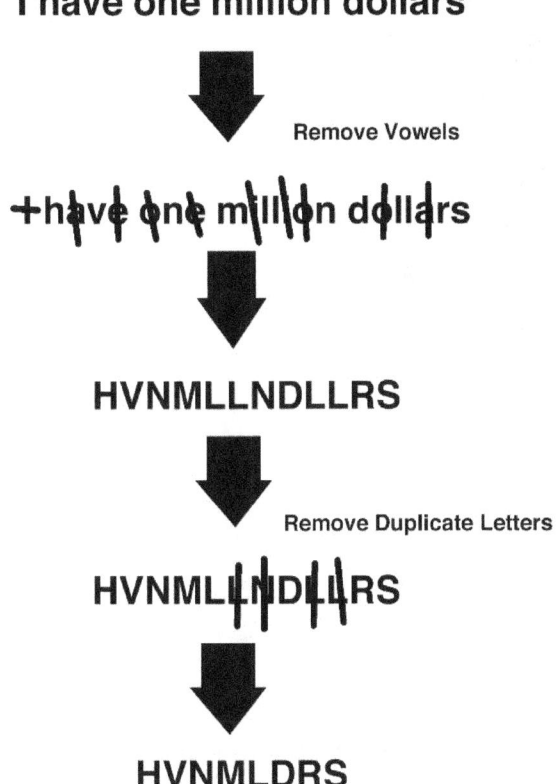

I have one million dollars

Remove Vowels

+h̶a̶v̶e̶ ̶o̶n̶e̶ m̶i̶l̶l̶i̶o̶n̶ d̶o̶l̶l̶a̶rs

HVNMLLNDLLRS

Remove Duplicate Letters

HVNML̶L̶N̶D̶L̶L̶RS

HVNMLDRS

Here's the resulting sigil created with those letters:

Nothing fancy, just a design using the letters. I whipped this up in Photoshop, but drawing this by hand is much more effective.

To take this further, you convert the letters to numbers, using any one of a number of translation methods. Once you have the letters converted, you map the numbers on a planetary square to generate a sigil based upon the magick of that planet!

My favorite is the use of the "Jewish Gematria":

Jewish Gematria

A=1	J=600	S=90
B=2	K=10	T=100
C=3	L=20	U=200
D=4	M=30	V=700
E=5	N=40	W=900
F=6	O=50	X=300
G=7	P=60	Y=400
H=8	Q=70	Z=500
I=9	R=80	

Thus, the letters "HVNMLDRS" will become

8, 700, 40, 30, 20, 4, 80, 90

If you look at the magick square of Jupiter, it only goes from 1-12, so you have to reduce the numbers to their lowest logical number. Thus, 700 becomes 7.

Now, we have 8,7,4,3,2,8,9

Overlay this on the Jupiter square:

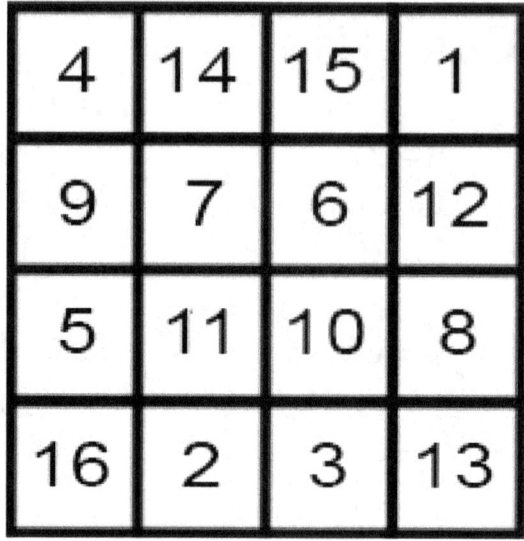

Draw a large dot over the letter 8, then a line to the rest of the numbers in order as shown.

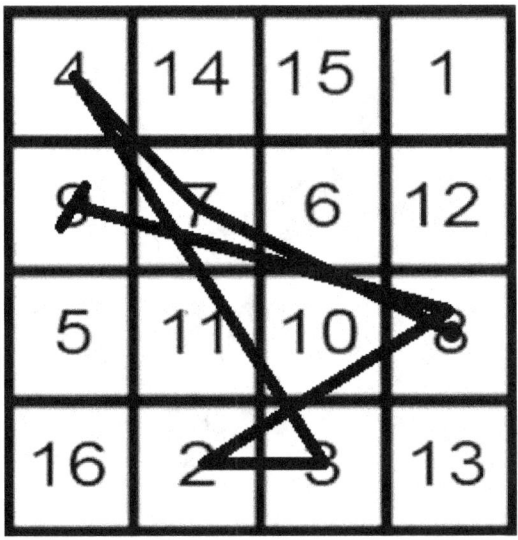

Then take the square away and you have the "working magic sigil"

David Thompson

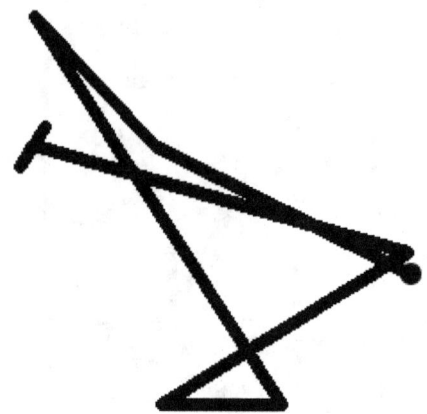

The various planetary squares are next.

THE *KAMEA* OF MERCURY
& PLANETARY SIGILS

8	58	59	5	4	62	63	1
49	15	14	52	53	11	10	56
41	23	22	44	45	19	18	48
32	34	35	29	28	38	39	25
40	26	27	37	36	30	31	33
17	47	46	20	21	43	42	24
9	55	54	12	13	51	50	16
64	2	3	61	60	6	7	57

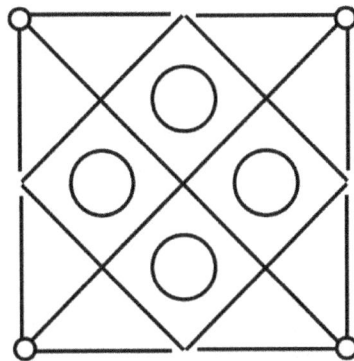

- Each row and column contains eight numbers
- The square contains 64 numbers from 1 to 64
- Each row, column and diagonal adds up to 260.
- All of the numbers in the square add up to 2080

THE *KAMEA* OF VENUS
& PLANETARY SIGILS

22	47	16	41	10	35	4
5	23	48	17	42	11	29
30	6	24	49	18	36	12
13	31	7	25	43	19	37
38	14	32	1	26	44	20
21	39	8	33	2	27	45
46	15	40	9	34	3	28

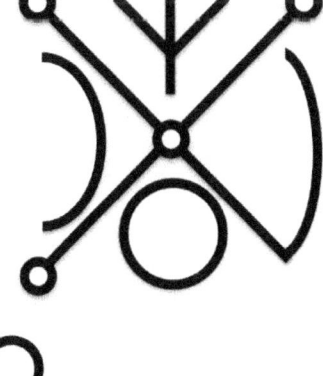

- Each row and column contains seven numbers
- The square contains 49 numbers from 1 to 49
- Each row, column and diagonal adds up to 175.
- All of the numbers in the square add up to 1225

149

THE *KAMEA* OF LUNA & PLANETARY SIGILS

37	78	29	70	21	62	13	54	5
6	38	79	30	71	22	63	14	46
47	7	39	80	31	72	23	55	15
16	48	8	40	81	32	64	24	56
57	17	49	9	41	73	33	65	25
26	58	18	50	1	42	74	34	66
67	27	59	10	51	2	43	75	35
36	68	19	60	11	52	3	44	76
77	28	69	20	61	12	53	4	45

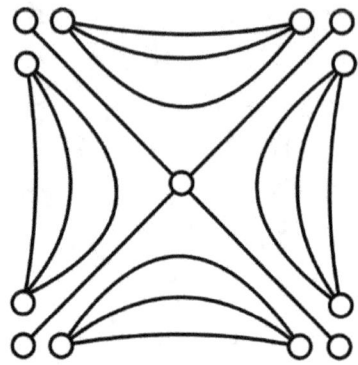

- Each row and column contains nine numbers
- The square contains 81 numbers from 1 to 81
- Each row, column and diagonal adds up to 260.
- All of the numbers in the square add up to 2080

THE KAMEA AND SIGIL OF MARS

11	24	7	20	3
4	12	25	8	16
17	5	13	21	9
10	18	1	14	22
23	6	19	2	15

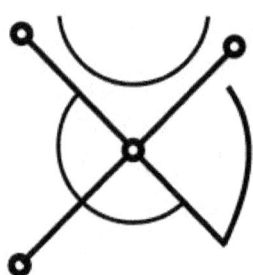

The Sigils or Seals of Mars

The *Kamea,* or Magic Square, of Mars, has the numbers 5, 25, 65, and 325 as its keys:
- Each row, column and diagonal has 5 squares.
- There are 25 boxes, holding 1 through 25
- Each row, column and diagonal adds to 65
- All the numbers add to 325

THE *KAMEA* OF JUPITER
& PLANETARY SIGILS

4	14	15	1
9	7	6	12
5	11	10	8
16	2	3	13

- Each row and column contains 4 numbers
- The square contains 16 numbers from 1 to 16
- Each row, column and diagonal adds up to 34.
- All of the numbers in the square add up to 136

The *Kamea* and Seal and Sign of Saturn

4	9	2
3	5	7
8	1	6

ד	ט	ב
ג	ה	ז
ח	א	ו

- Each row and column contains three numbers
- The square contains 9 numbers from 1 to 9
- Each row, column and diagonal adds up to 15.
- All of the numbers in the square add up to 45

THE *KAMEA* OF THE SUN
& PLANETARY SIGILS

6	32	3	34	35	1
7	11	27	28	8	30
19	14	16	15	23	24
18	20	22	21	17	13
25	29	10	9	26	12
36	5	33	4	2	31

- Each row and column contains six numbers.
- The square contains 36 numbers from 1 to 36.
- Each row, column and diagonal adds up to 111.
- All of the numbers in the square add up to 666.

Creating a Talisman

You can have the Master Sigil turned into a nice piece of jewelry, something to carry with you. I know of an artist who excels in this and he comes highly recommended. A link is at the end of this section.

A talisman is a physical piece, usually of a sigil, that possess the power to draw to you what you wish to manifest. Just about any sigil can be turned into a talisman of most any size. I have found that a 2-inch (5 cm) disc is just about perfect for a key-fob. Slightly smaller for a pendant, and up to 4 inches (10cm) for an altar piece.

If you cannot afford to turn the Master Sigil (or any sigil) into a solid talisman, you can draw a sigil on a disc of wood, or have the paper sigil laminated to some thick card stock.

Charging a Talisman

Once you have the physical talisman, it needs to be "charged", energized before it'll start working. This is a simply ritual where you summon the Daemonic spokesman and the talisman is charged by injecting with energy and asking the being to energize the talisman, then hold the talisman over some frankincense and you're done.

The Pendulum

Don't happen to have a Pendulum? No worries! No sense in making this harder than it is. Don't over think. Just make a pendulum!

A pendulum can be made from most anything. All you really need is a length of string or jewelry chain, and something to tie at the bottom.

You can use a ring, a small stone, or even a house key.

Just attach the ring or key to the end of the string or chain, and TA DAH! A pendulum! Wasn't that EASY? Simpler *IS* better!

Activating and Charging your Pendulum

Before working the ritual that uses a pendulum, let's first consecrate the pendulum.

To do this, place the pendulum on your workspace and hold your hands over it.

Imagine a light entering your head and flowing into your hands, then into the pendulum.

Now say:

In the name of EH-EI-EH I ask you, Angel METATRON to bless this pendulum and shape its energies for spirit communication with Genius entities. Make it safe for myself while I use this pendulum. So be it! Amein! (That

last work is Hebraic for So be IT)

Now, your pendulum is ready for use.

DAVID THOMPSON

Pendulum Charts

Alphabet Chart

DAVID THOMPSON

Yes/No Chart

Write in your own answers

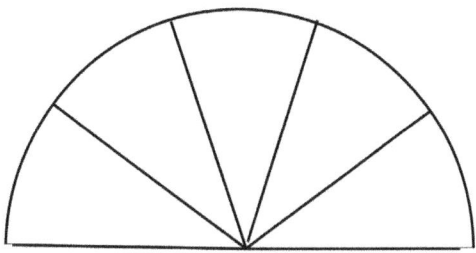

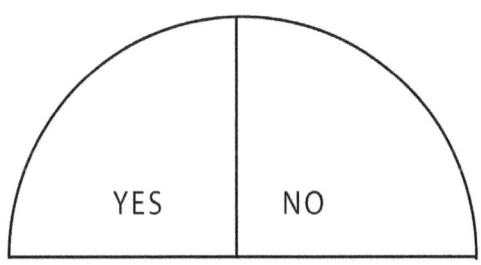

YES   NO

Pendulum Wheel Dates

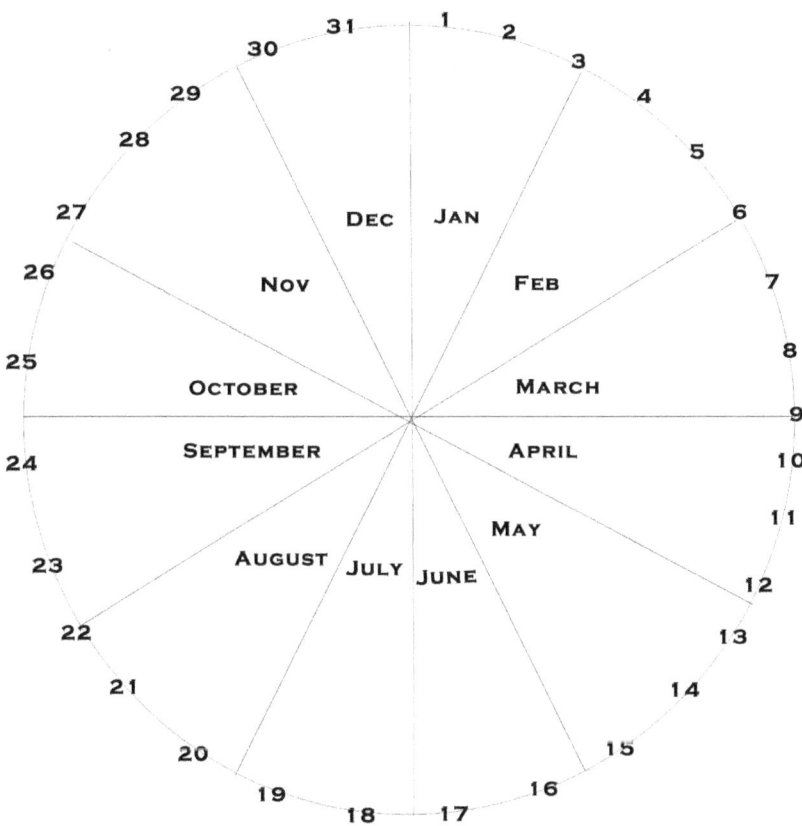

Full size charts available online – see the links.

DAVID THOMPSON

Candles and Candle Safety

There are fires caused by unattended candles almost every week. People have lost their lives in fires started by unattended candles.

I have had a close call when a candle burned low and caught its label on fire. I saw it in time and put the thing out. I have seen 7-day votive candles filled with herbs begin to "torch", the herbs burning so that the entire top of the candle is on fire.

Some other rituals suggest you add crushed herbs or ground spices to a candle. This is okay as long as it's a taper or pillar candle where the bits can fall away while the candle burns. If you are using a glass enclosed votive candle, these will collect in the melted wax near the flame and catch fire, creating a second or third wick. I have seen these candles look like torches as the herbs caught fire. The crushed herbs will not burn, *they will act as wicks*, burning the wax and not completely burning themselves. Once the top of the candle is aflame, the glass is likely to shatter due to the concentrated heat. When the glass shatters, the hot wax and burning herbs will drop to the table. Then you have a serious problem.

And never use water to put out a candle fire. Smother it with a wet towel or use a fire extinguisher. Water will splatter the burning wax and make things much, much worse.

If using votive candles, do not use dried herbs or spices. Use essential oils of those herbs. The oil will behave itself.

The rituals in this book use a specific candle called the Spell Candle. These smaller candles must burn away to finish the ritual.

So I burn them in heavy holders with foil linings. I also place the burning candle far away from anything else that can catch fire if the holder cracks.

ABOUT THE AUTHOR

Dave is an author of adult fantasy (The Furies series) as well as author of occult books about magick.

David began working ritual magick back in the 1970s. He took a brief break, then used the power of this magick to create a photography career which took him to Los Angeles and work as a photographer for multiple magazines.

David has studied magick in all forms, and in 2018, released a three-part magick instruction course in High Magick. Thousands of students have benefited from David's unique teaching style, making ceremonial magick accessible to everyone.

Daemons of Fortune is book 6 in his High Magick Series.

Dave also has a series on Grecian Magick, exploring the aspects of ceremonial magick with the gods and goddesses of ancient Greece.

Dave's Facebook Page:

https://www.facebook.com/DavePsychic/

Secrets of Magick Facebook Group:

https://www.facebook.com/groups/secretsofmagick

Join the Grecian and High Magick Books Facebook group!

Https://www.facebook.com/groups/grecianhighmagick/

And finally, Dave's webpage, book readings and his services:

https://davepsychic.com

Sign-up for my Newsletter and get a FREE E-Book!

https://davepsychic.com/newsletter

Magick Books by David Thompson

Available on Kindle, Paperback and Hardcover (*). All links lead to the Kindle version.

High Magick Series

- ☐ High Magick 101
- ☐ Daemons of High Magick
- ☐ Daemons and the Law of Attraction
- ☐ Magick of Astaroth
- ☐ Lilith: Goddess of Darkness and Light
- ☐ High Magick Workbook (paperback only)

High Magick supplemental material

- ☐ Tarot Reading Logbook (Paperback only)
- ☐ Tarot Journal: Power of the Tarot (Paperback Only)
- ☐ Book of Shadows: A Personal Grimoire (Paperback only)

Grecian Magick Series

- ☐ Magick of Apollo
- ☐ Magick of Hermes
- ☐ Magick of Aphrodite
- ☐ Magick of Fortuna
- ☐ Greco-Roman Wealth Magick
- ☐ Magick of the Sirens/Magick of the Muses

Fiction Novels by David Thompson

The Furies Series

- ☐ Angels of Vengeance
- ☐ Descent into Tartarus
- ☐ Furies: Beginnings
- ☐ Brianna: Making of a Fury